D0723622

INTELEXUAL MEDIA

How To Use This Book

Most black quotes used on media sites or showcased during Black History Month are generic or oft repeated. That is not the case with ***Who Said Dat?: 500 Black A** Quotes From Intellectuals, Historical Figures, Celebs, and Everyday People***. This book has plenty of gems. I have been casually collecting these quotes for the past six months in a word document on my computer. If you, the person reading this book, were a student in my hypothetical classroom, there are a few tasks I'd assign to you to make sure that these words are not only read but studied. The tasks?

- **Read Blindly:** I didn't sort quotes in this book into categories or by the author because I didn't want you, the reader, to skim past a name or topic you don't find relevant or refreshing. Read each quote in full before letting your eyes find the author's name between the parenthesis. Judge the words before deciding if you like it or not because of who said it.

- **Verify Context:** Quotes have a funny way of being used in unintended ways. This often happens when someone reads a quote without seeing why the original orator even formulated the words. With that being said, searching for these quotes on google will bring forth interesting sources that will help you critique these words with nuance. What historical events were happening at the time that a particular quote occurred? Is the quote in question commenting on past events or is it a primary source?

- **Verify Credibility:** People often say one thing and do another. When reading these quotes, skimming the biographies of the speakers will allow for a fuller understanding of if their words were the real McCoy.

- **Create Categories:** If you love annotating and highlighting like I do, this one is for you. After skimming through this book, contrive 6-8 color-coded categories to sort quotes into with highlighters or pens. Example categories include Slave Narratives, Fighting Words, On Black Womanhood, On Black Manhood, On Racism, Education, and Pop Culture.

- **Feel Free To Disagree:** Once you gain context of a quote in this book, you may discover you don't like it. That's okay. Write a response or challenge its validity. One of the most fun parts of studying history is formulating your own informed opinions.

But, as I'm not your actual teacher and can't make sure you use this book to expand your personal journey into black history, the utilization of these pages is really up to you. Some of these quotes are funny. Some are sad. A small portion is not politically or socially significant. Some are profound. Others are just trifling. But they were all said or written by black people.

Without further ado, in no particular order, here are ***500 Black A** Quotes From Intellectuals, Historical Figures, Celebs, and Everyday People.***

1. I am sick and tired of being sick and tired. (Fannie Lou Hamer)
2. If the white man gives you anything - just remember when he gets ready he will take it right back. We have to take for ourselves (Fannie Lou Hamer)
3. Racism is still with us. But it is up to us to prepare our children for what they have to meet, and, hopefully, we shall overcome." (Rosa Parks)
4. If the white man gives you anything - just remember when he gets ready he will take it right back. We have to take for ourselves. (Fannie Lou Hamer)
5. 'All I remember is that I was not going to walk off the bus voluntarily,' said Claudette Colvin when discussing the March 2nd 1955 incident (nine months before Rosa Parks) in which she refused to give up her seat to a white woman. My head was just too full of black history, you know, the oppression that we went through. It felt like Sojourner Truth was on one side pushing me down, and Harriet Tubman was on the other side of me pushing me down. I couldn't get up. (*Claudette Colvin: Twice Towards Justice* by Phillip Hoose)
6. As a black woman, my politics and political affiliation are bound up with and flow from participation in my people's struggle for liberation, and with the fight of oppressed people all over the world against American imperialism. (Angela Davis)

7. Yes, I think it's really important to acknowledge that Dr. King, precisely at the moment of his assassination, was re-conceptualizing the civil rights movement and moving toward a sort of coalitional relationship with the trade union movement. (Angela Davis)
8. My activism did not spring from my being gay, or, for that matter, from my being black. Rather, it is rooted fundamentally in my Quaker upbringing and the values that were instilled in me by my grandparents who reared me. (Bayard Rustin)
9. Martin Luther King, with whom I worked very closely, became very distressed when a number of the ministers working for him wanted him to dismiss me from his staff because of my homosexuality. (Bayard Rustin)
10. Our grandfathers had to run, run, run. My generation's out of breath. We ain't running no more. (Stokely Carmichael)
11. I also know that while I am black I am a human being, and therefore I have the right to go into any public place. White people didn't know that. Every time I tried to go into a place they stopped me. (Stokely Carmichael)
12. Before a group can enter the open society, it must first close ranks.(Stokely Carmichael)
13. There has been only a civil rights movement, whose tone of voice was adapted to an audience of liberal whites. (Stokely Carmichael)

14. No nation, savage or civilized, save only the United States of America, has confessed its inability to protect its women save by hanging, shooting, and burning alleged offenders. (Ida B. Wells)
15. The appeal to the white man's pocket has ever been more effectual than all the appeals ever made to his conscience.(Ida B. Wells)
16. The city of Memphis has demonstrated that neither character nor standing avails the Negro if he dares to protect himself against the white man or become his rival (Ida B. Wells in 1892 when urging black people to leave the city after a lynch mob killed three of her friends)
17. There's only one free person in this society, and he is white and male. (Hazel Scott)
18. We've never advocated violence; violence is inflicted upon us. But we do believe in self-defense for ourselves and for black people. (Huey Newton)
19. I believe I'm going to die doing the things I was born to do. I believe I'm going to die high off the people. I believe I'm going to die a revolutionary in the international revolutionary proletarian struggle.(Fred Hampton)
20. We're going to fight racism not with racism, but we're going to fight with solidarity. We say we're not going to fight capitalism with black capitalism, but we're going to fight it with socialism. (Fred Hampton)

21. I believe in the brotherhood of all men, but I don't believe in wasting brotherhood on anyone who doesn't want to practice it with me. Brotherhood is a two-way street. (Malcolm X)
22. The media's the most powerful entity on earth. They have the power to make the innocent guilty and to make the guilty innocent, and that's power. Because they control the minds of the masses. (Malcolm X)
23. The goal of Dr. Martin Luther King is to give Negroes a chance to sit in a segregated restaurant beside the same white man who had brutalized them for 400 years. (Malcolm X)
24. We won't organize any black man to be a Democrat or a Republican because both of them have sold us out. Both of them have sold us out; both parties have sold us out. Both parties are racist, and the Democratic Party is more racist than the Republican Party. (Malcolm X)
25. A hoodie is worn by everybody: kids, white men, white women, black men. But it clings to the black body as a sign of criminality like nothing else.(Claudia Rankine)
26. Sometimes, you feel like, 'Am I going to be upset about this as a black person or as a woman first? Or am I gonna be both?' Because some things inherently affect black women; some things affect you as a woman and not a black person; and some things just affect you as a black person. (Jessica Williams)
27. Any film I do is not going to change the way black women

have been portrayed, or black people have been portrayed, in cinema since the days of D.W. Griffith.(Spike Lee)

28. The South is very beautiful but its beauty makes one sad because the lives that people live here, and have lived here, are so ugly. (James Baldwin)
29. It is only in his music, which Americans are able to admire because a protective sentimentality limits their understanding of it, that the Negro in America has been able to tell his story. (James Baldwin)
30. The reason people think it's important to be white is that they think it's important not to be black. (James Baldwin)
31. So much has been written about me, and people don't know what's right and what's wrong. I'd rather let them stay confused. (Prince)
32. People say I'm wearing heels because I'm short. I wear heels because the women like 'em.(Prince)
33. Like books and black lives, albums still matter. (Prince)
34. It's not enough even to have one black Barbie... because black women are not a monolith. (Ava DuVernay)
35. Black women sharing close ties with each other, politically or emotionally, are not the enemies of Black men. (Audre Lorde)
36. There is a great stir about colored men getting their rights, but not a word about the colored women; and if colored men get their rights, and not colored women theirs, you see, the

colored men will be masters over the women, and it will be just as bad as it was before. (Sojourner Truth)

37. That I am a national figure because I was the first person in 192 years to be at once a congressman, black, and a woman proves, I would think, that our society is not yet either just or free. (Shirley Chisolm)
38. I had to get through this. There would be no second chance to get through A this. I noticed that none of Emmett s body was scarred. It was bloated, the skin was loose, but there were no scars, no signs of violence anywhere. Until I got to his chin. When I got to his chin, I saw his tongue resting there. It was huge. I never imagined that a human tongue could be that big. Maybe it was the effect of the water, since he had been in the river for several days, or maybe the heat. But as I gazed at the tongue, I couldn't help but think that it had been choked out of his mouth. I forced myself to move on, to keep going one small section at a time, as if taking this gruesome task in small doses could somehow make it less excruciating. . . . From the chin I moved up to his right cheek. There was an eyeball hanging down, resting on that cheek everyone always thought was so pretty. Right away, I looked to the other eye. But it wasn't there. It seemed like someone had taken a nut picker and plucked that one out. . . . [His nose] had been chopped, maybe with a meat cleaver. It looked as if someone had tenderized his nose." (Mamie Till Mobley's words in

Behold the Corpse: Violent Images and the Case of Emmett Till by Christine Harold and Kevin Michael DeLuca)

39. I did not tell you that it would be okay, because I have never believed it would be okay. What I told you is what your grandparents tried to tell me: that this is your country, that this is your world, that this is your body, and you must find some way to live within the all of it. (Ta-Nehisi Coates)
40. Anyone who has ever struggled with poverty knows how extremely expensive it is to be poor. (James Baldwin)
41. If they don't give you a seat at the table, bring a folding chair. (Shirley Chisolm)
42. Holocaust survivors and their descendants are supposed to hate those who oppressed and killed them and their people. Black people are not. This is how anti-blackness works. (Darnell Lamont Walker)
43. Though the colored man is no longer subject to be bought and sold, he is still surrounded by an adverse sentiment which fetters all his movements. In his downward course he meets with no resistance, but his course upward is resented and resisted at every step of his progress. If he comes in ignorance, rags, and wretchedness, he conforms to the popular belief of his character, and in that character he is welcome. But if he shall come as a gentleman, a scholar, and a statesman, he is hailed as a contradiction to the national faith concerning his race, and his coming is resented as impudence.

In the one case he may provoke contempt and derision, but in the other he is an affront to pride and provokes malice. Let him do what he will, there is at present, therefore, no escape for him. The color line meets him everywhere, and in a measure shuts him out from all respectable and profitable trades and callings. (Fredrick Douglass)

44. I have nothing to do with racism in America; it was here when I got here. (Paul Mooney)
45. We have a lot of black Anglo-Saxons. Their skin is black, but their brain is white. When I get real mad at them, I call them 'graham crackers.' (Paul Mooney)
46. If you have money and you have fame, but you don't have any confidence in your blackness, then it's all for nothing. (Paul Mooney)
47. The American Negro never can be blamed for his racial animosities - he is only reacting to 400 years of the conscious racism of the American whites. (Malcolm X)
48. I had a vision - and I saw white spirits and black spirits engaged in battle, and the sun was darkened - the thunder rolled in the Heavens, and blood flowed in streams - and I heard a voice saying, 'Such is your luck, such are you called to see, and let it come rough or smooth, you must surely bear it.' (Nat Turner)
49. "Sometimes, I feel discriminated against, but it does not make me angry. It merely astonishes me. How can any deny

themselves the pleasure of my company? It's beyond me." (Zora Neale Hurston)

50. There is always something to do. There are hungry people to feed, naked people to clothe, sick people to comfort and make well. And while I don't expect you to save the world I do think it's not asking too much for you to love those with whom you sleep, share the happiness of those whom you call friend, engage those among you who are visionary and remove from your life those who offer you depression, despair and disrespect. (Nikki Giovanni)
51. I had reasoned this out in my mind, there was one of two things I had a right to two things, liberty or death; if I could not have one, I would have the other. (Harriet Tubman)
52. I am a woman who came from the cotton fields of the South. From there I was promoted to the washtub. From there I was promoted to the cook kitchen. And from there I promoted myself into the business of manufacturing hair goods and preparations....I have built my own factory on my own ground. (Madam C.J. Walker)
53. Oddly, I had never thought of myself as a feminist. I had been denounced by certain radical feminist collectives as a 'lackey' for men. That charge was based on my having written and sung two albums of songs that my female accusers claimed elevated and praised men. Resenting that label, I had joined the majority of black women in America in denouncing femi-

nism… . The feminists were right. The value of my life had been obliterated as much by being female as by being black and poor. Racism and sexism in America were equal partners in my oppression." (Elaine Brown)

54. People called me a hoodlum and a thug. But they didn't tell you I was a carpenter, an architect, a stand-up comic - even a bartender. And a barbecue cook. But they didn't tell you that. (Bobby Seale)
55. People have been murdered for less than what the Black Panthers did, so the question was for us: 'Do you want to live on your knees or die on your feet?'. (Kathleen Cleaver)
56. To develop political and economic power in a capitalist society, you need capital. (Bobby Seale)
57. "I'd rather see him take a knee than stand up, put his hands up and get murdered. My take on it is, [stuff], it got to start somewhere and if that was the starting point, I just hope people open up their eyes and see that it's really a problem going on and something needs to be done for it to stop. If you really not racist, then you won't see what [Kaepernick is] doing as a threat to America, but just addressing a problem that we have." (Marshawn Lynch)
58. My mother said I must always be intolerant of ignorance but understanding of illiteracy. That some people, unable to go to school, were more intelligent and more educated than college professors. (Maya Angelou)

59. Black people are not the descendants of kings. We are—and I say this with big pride—the progeny of slaves. If there's any majesty in our struggle, it lies not in fairy tales but in those humble origins and the great distance we've traveled since. Ditto for the dreams of a separate but noble past. Cosby's, and much of black America's, conservative analysis flattens history and smooths over the wrinkles that have characterized black America since its inception. (Ta-Nehisi Coates)
60. "By the turn of the twentieth century, every state in the South had laws on the books that disenfranchised blacks and discriminated against them in virtually ever sphere of life, lending sanction to a racial ostracism that extended to schools, churches, housing, jobs, restrooms, hotels, restaurants, hospitals, orphanages, prisons, funeral homes, morgues, and cemeteries. Politicians competed with each other by proposing and passing every more stringent, oppressive, and downright ridiculous legislation (such as laws specifically prohibiting blacks and whites from playing chess together.)" (Michelle Alexander)
61. People look at me like I should have been like Malcolm X or Martin Luther King or Rosa Parks. I should have seen life like that and stay out of trouble, and don't do this and don't do that. But it's hard to live up to some people's expectations. (Rodney King)
62. I'm not quite sure what freedom is, but i know damn well

what it ain't. How have we gotten so silly, I wonder. (Assata Shakur)

63. Within the lesbian community I am Black, and within the Black community I am a lesbian. Any attack against Black people is a lesbian and gay issue, because I and thousands of other Black women are part of the lesbian community. Any attack against lesbians and gays is a Black issue, because thousands of lesbians and gay men are Black. There is no hierarchy of oppression. (Audre Lorde)
64. You don't get black power by chanting it. You get it by doing what the other groups have done. The Irish kept quiet. They didn't shout "Irish Power", "Jew Power", [or] "Italian Power". They kept their mouths shut and took over the police department of New York City, and the mayorship of Boston. (Whitney M. Young)
65. "Don't you know that slavery was outlawed?" "No," the guard said, "you're wrong. Slavery was outlawed with the exception of prisons. Slavery is legal in prisons." I looked it up and sure enough, she was right. The Thirteenth Amendment to the Constitution says: "Neither slavery nor involuntary servitude, except as a punishment for crime whereof the party shall have been duly convicted, shall exist within the United States, or any place subject to their jurisdiction." Well, that explained a lot of things. That explained why jails and prisons all over the country are filled to the brim with Black and Third World

people, why so many Black people can't find a job on the streets and are forced to survive the best way they know how. Once you're in prison, there are plenty of jobs, and, if you don't want to work, they beat you up and throw you in a hole. If every state had to pay workers to do the jobs prisoners are forced to do, the salaries would amount to billions… Prisons are a profitable business. They are a way of legally perpetuating slavery. In every state more and more prisons are being built and even more are on the drawing board. Who are they for? They certainly aren't planning to put white people in them. Prisons are part of this government's genocidal war against Black and Third World people." (Assata Shakur)

66. It is easy to romanticize poverty, to see poor people as inherently lacking agency and will. It is easy to strip them of human dignity, to reduce them to objects of pity. This has never been clearer than in the view of Africa from the American media, in which we are shown poverty and conflicts without any context. (Chimamanda Ngozi Adichie)
67. Schools in amerika are interested in brainwashing people with amerikanism, giving them a little bit of education, and training them in skills needed to fill the positions the capitalist system requires. As long as we expect amerika's schools to educate us, we will remain ignorant. (Assata Shakur)
68. I am for violence if non-violence means we continue postponing a solution to the American black man's problem just

to avoid violence. (Malcolm X)

69. The schools we go to are reflections of the society that created them. Nobody is going to give you the education you need to overthrow them. Nobody is going to teach you your true history, teach you your true heroes, if they know that that knowledge will help set you free. (Assata Shakur)
70. Things like racism are institutionalized. You might not know any bigots. You feel like "well I don't hate black people so I'm not a racist," but you benefit from racism. Just by the merit, the color of your skin. The opportunities that you have, you're privileged in ways that you might not even realize because you haven't been deprived of certain things. We need to talk about these things in order for them to change. (Dave Chappelle)
71. A people without the knowledge of their past history, origin and culture is like a tree without roots. (Marcus Garvey)
72. I regard the Klan, the Anglo-Saxon clubs and White American societies, as far as the Negro is concerned, as better friends of the race than all other groups of hypocritical whites put together. (Marcus Garvey)
73. You were born where you were born and faced the future that you faced because you were black and for no other reason. The limits of your ambition were, thus, expected to be set forever. You were born into a society which spelled out with brutal clarity, and in as many ways as possible, that you were

a worthless human being. You are not expected to aspire to excellence: you were expected to make peace with mediocrity. (James Baldwin)

74. People know about the Klan and the overt racism, but the killing of one's soul little by little, day after day, is a lot worse than someone coming in your house and lynching you. (Samuel L Jackson)
75. Those Garveyites I knew could never understand why I liked them but would never follow them, and I pitied them too much to tell them that they could never achieve their goal, that Africa was owned by the imperial powers of Europe, that their lives were alien to the mores of the natives of Africa, that they were people of the West and would for ever be so until they either merged with the West or perished. (Richard Wright)
76. If men could get pregnant, abortion would be a sacrament. (Florynce Kennedy)
77. Everybody's scared for their ass. There aren't too many people ready to die for racism. They'll kill for racism but they won't die for racism. (Florynce Kennedy)
78. Men simply copied the realities of their hearts when they built prisons. (Richard Wright)
79. The drums of Africa still beat in my heart. They will not let me rest while there is a single Negro boy or girl without a chance to prove his worth. (Mary McLeod Bethune)

80. The fight against male chauvinism is a class struggle— that's hard for people to understand. To understand male chauvinism one has to understand that is it inter-locked with racism. Male chauvinism is directly related through the notion of sexual differences by race. Cultural nationalists, like Ron Karenga, are male chauvinists as well. What they do is oppress the black woman. Their black racism leads them to theories of male domination as well. Thus black racists come to the same conclusions that white racists do with respect to their women. The party says no to this. Personally, I don't think that women who want liberation want penises — they just want to be treated as human beings on an equal basis, just as blacks who demand the liberation of their people. Eldridge Cleaver talked about this in "Soul on Ice." Superman never tries to relate to Lois Lane, nor does he try to relate to the oppressed. Rather he relates to superficial violence, throwing people halfway across the ocean, etc. The concept I'm trying to establish is the cross-relation of male chauvinism to any other form of chauvinism—including racism. In other words the idea of saying "keep a woman in her place" is only a short step away from saying "keep a nigger in his place." As Eldridge said in his book, the white woman is a symbol of freedom in this country. The white man took this chick and stuck her up on a pedestal and called her the Statue of Liberty and gave her a torch to hold. Well I say put a ma-

chine gun in her other hand. (Bobby Seale)

81. I remembered how tough it was getting black people in large tenements to come together to build a playground. The enemy was not the Klan by the inside-outside lock that racism and classism had on the minds of the people: It operated from the inside through self-hate and self-doubt, and from the outside through the police, carnivorous landlords, and the welfare system. (Junius Williams in *Unfinished Agenda: Urban Politics in the Era of Black Power*)
82. Racism as a form of skin worship, and as a sickness and a pathological anxiety for America, is so great, until the poor whites -- rather than fighting for jobs or education -- fight to remain pink and fight to remain white. And therefore they cannot see an alliance with people that they feel to be inherently inferior. (Jesse Jackson)
83. For many years, I believed racism in America was dead and that opportunity existed for all. My beliefs were shaken when the Rodney King officers were acquitted. (John Hope Bryant)
84. What kind of motivated me to join the Black Panther Party was that I, along with some of the comrades that I was working with in New York, had heard about the Black Panther Party, and they were doing things that we wanted to do in New York, and we thought that would be a better vehicle than the vehicle that we had going on in New York. They were better organized, and they already had their Ten-Point

Platform and Program, and people already heard about them. So we decided that we would join the party, when given a chance. (Sekou Odinga)

85. I think because I came into journalism by way of the Black Panther Party - and not J-school or a corporate bourgeois institution - I tried to do news, writing and reporting that had social, political and racial content and context. (Mumia Abu Jamal)
86. That was one of the big problems in the [Black Panther] Party. Criticism and self-criticism were not encouraged, and the little that was given often wasn't taken seriously. Constructive criticism and self-criticism are extremely important for any revolutionary organization. Without them, people tend to drown in their mistakes, not learn from them. (Assata Shakur)
87. It comes down to this: black people were stripped of our identities when we were brought here, and it's been a quest since then to define who we are. (Spike Lee)
88. Dr. King's policy was that nonviolence would achieve the gains for black people in the United States. His major assumption was that if you are nonviolent, if you suffer, your opponent will see your suffering and will be moved to change his heart. That's very good. He only made one fallacious assumption: In order for nonviolence to work, your opponent must have a conscience. The United States has none. (Stokely

Carmichael)

89. I felt that one had better die fighting against injustice than to die like a dog or rat in a trap. I had already determined to sell my life as dearly as possible if attacked. I felt if I could take one lyncher with me, this would even up the score a little bit. (Ida B. Wells)
90. Jim Crow is alive and it's dressed in a Brooks Brothers suit, my friend, instead of a white robe. (Myrlie Evers WIlliams)
91. Everyday, day & night, we hear the lies that September 11th is the worst tragedy, worst accident, and worst crime to ever been committed on American soil. We bear witness that the worst crime, the worst tragedy, that has ever taken place on American soil is not September 11th. It's not the twin towers. It's the holocaust that black folks been dealing with for 400 years. (Malik Zulu Shabazz)
92. Two months ago I had a nice apartment in Chicago. I had a good job. I had a son. When something happened to the Negroes in the South I said, `That's their business, not mine.' Now I know how wrong. I was. The murder of my son has shown me that what happens to any of us, anywhere in the world, had better be the business of us all. (Mamie Till Mobley)
93. I freed a thousand slaves I could have freed a thousand more if only they knew they were slaves. (Harriet Tubman)
94. I am America. I am the part you won't recognize. But get

used to me. Black, confident, cocky; my name, not yours; my religion, not yours; my goals, my own; get used to me. (Muhammad Ali)

95. George Bush doesn't care about black people. (Kanye West)
96. Black people dominate sports in the United States. 20% of the population and 90% of the final four. (Chris Rock)
97. I know I got it made while the masses of black people are catchin' hell, but as long as they ain't free, I ain't free. (Muhammad Ali)
98. Black people know what white people mean when they say "law and order." (Fannie Lou Hammer)
99. America will tolerate the taking of a human life without giving it a second thought. But don't misuse a household pet. (Dick Gregory)
100. It is necessary to understand that Black Power is a cry of disappointment. The Black Power slogan did not spring full grown from the head of some philosophical Zeus. It was born from the wounds of despair and disappointment. It is a cry of daily hurt and persistent pain. (Martin Luther King Jr)
101. The civil rights movement didn't deal with the issue of political disenfranchisement in the Northern cities. It didn't deal with the issues that were happening in Northern cities like Detroit, where there was a deep process of deindustrialization going on. So you have this response of angry young people, with a war going on in Vietnam, a poverty program

that was insufficient, and police brutality. All these things gave rise to the Black Power Movement. It was not a separation from the civil rights movement, but a continuum of this whole process of democratization. (Danny Glover)

102. When I dare to be powerful - to use my strength in the service of my vision, then it becomes less and less important whether I am afraid. (Audre Lorde)

103. I do think it's extremely important to acknowledge the gains that were made by the civil rights movement, the black power movement.Institutional transformations happened directly as a result of the movements that people, unnamed people, organized and gave their lives to. (Angela Davis)

104. The lesson this teaches and which every Afro-American should ponder well, is that a Winchester rifle should have a place of honor in every black home, and it should be used for that protection which the law refuses to give. When the white man who is always the aggressor knows he runs as great a risk of biting the dust every time his Afro-American victim does, he will have greater respect for Afro-American life. The more the Afro-American yields and cringes and begs, the more he has to do so, the more he is insulted, outraged and lynched. (Ida B Wells)

105. We need to eradicate the slander that says a black youth with a book is acting white. (Barack Obama)

106. Hip hop music is important precisely because it sheds

light on contemporary politics, history, and race. At its best, hip hop gives voice to marginal black youth we are not used to hearing from on such topics. (Michael Eric Dyson)

107. As far as I knew white women were never lonely, except in books. White men adored them, Black men desired them and Black women worked for them. (Maya Angelou)

108. The most disrespected person in America is the black woman. The most unprotected person in America is the black woman. The most neglected person in America is the black woman. (Malcolm X)

109. I know black women in Tennessee who have worked all their lives, from the time they were twelve years old to the day they died. These women don't listen to the women's liberation rhetoric because they know that it's nothing but a bunch of white women who had certain life-styles and who want to change those life-styles. (Wilma Rudolph)

110. The issue of redistribution of resources and wealth needs to resolved systemically, but in the meantime but there are individual spots you can occupy. There are things that you can do on a daily basis that will make a difference in moving the needle in individual lives. When we look at the mentoring of young black kids, for instance, the number-one mentor group is white women. I think after that maybe it's black women, and then white men, and then black men. We can make all kinds of arguments about that. (Michael Eric Dyson)

111. Black Power simply means: Look at me, I'm here. I have dignity. I have pride. I have roots. I insist, I demand that I participate in those decisions that affect my life and the lives of my children. It means that I am somebody. (Whitney M. Young)

112. Black Girl Magic is a radiant revolution against misogynoir - misogyny directed towards Black women and internalized hatred. Black women are subject to so many societal messages that tell them they are not beautiful, smart, or capable. Black Girl Magic is the conscious unraveling of those toxic concepts through self-love and acceptance. It preaches that despite the pressures I face, I glow more than ever before. (Amandla Stenberg)

113. No woman on this whole earth can please me and cook for me and socialise and talk to me like my American black woman. (Muhammad Ali)

114. Men who are proud of being black marry black women; women who are proud of being black marry black men. (Malcolm X)

115. I'm not angry. And I don't like the thing of the 'angry black woman,' either. (Naomi Campbell)

116. I go out with white women. This makes a lot of people unhappy, mostly black women. (Dennis Rodman)

117. I want history to remember me... not as the first black woman to have made a bid for the presidency of the United

States, but as a black woman who lived in the 20th century and who dared to be herself. I want to be remembered as a catalyst for change in America. (Shirley Chisolm)

118. They wanted black women to conform to the gender norms set by white society. They wanted to be recognized as 'men,' as patriarchs, by other men, including white men. Yet they could not assume this position if black women were not willing to conform to prevailing sexist gender norms. Many black women who has endured white-supremacist patriarchal domination during slavery did not want to be dominated by black men after manumission. (bell hooks)

119. As for those who think the Arab world promises freedom, the briefest study of its routine traditional treatment of blacks (slavery) and women (purdah) will provide relief from all illusion. If Malcolm X had been a black woman his last message to the world would have been entirely different. The brotherhood of Moslem men-all colors-may exist there, but part of the glue that holds them together is the thorough suppression of women. (Alice Walker)

120. True the Black woman did the housework, the drudgery; true, she reared the children, often alone, but she did all of that while occupying a place on the job market, a place her mate could not get or which his pride would not let him accept.And she had nothing to fall back on: not maleness, not whiteness, not ladyhood, not anything. And out of the

profound desolation of her reality she may very well have invented herself. (Toni Morrison)

121. I just like to have words that describe things correctly. Now to me, 'black feminist' does not do that. I need a word that is organic, that really comes out of the culture, that really expresses the spirit that we see in black women. And it's just... womanish. (Alice Walker)

122. Don't terrorize. Organize. Don't burn. Give kids a chance to learn . . . The real answer to race problems in this country is education. Not burning and killing. Be ready. Be qualified. Own something. Be somebody. That's Black Power. (James Brown)

123. Having Black hair is unique in that Black women change up styles a lot. You can walk down one street block in New York City and see 10 different hairstyles that Black women are wearing: straight curls, short cuts, braids - we really run the gamut. (Queen Latifah)

124. Whenever black women have a point, they're characterized as angry black women, and therefore the thing they're talking about is no longer of importance because they have to deal with them being overly emotional or something. I recognize that people who respond negatively to what I have to say aren't at a place yet where they are able to learn ... And it's exactly what I'm trying to fight. (Amandla Stenberg)

125. ... Not all black women have silently acquiesced in sexism

and misogyny within the African-American community. Indeed, many writers, activists, and other women have voiced their opposition and paid the price: they have been ostracized and branded as either man- haters or pawns of white feminists, two of the more predictable modes of disciplining and discrediting black feminists. (Kimberle Williams Crenshaw)

126. Obama, he wouldn't have been in office without what happened to me and a lot of black people before me. He would never have been in that situation, no doubt in my mind. He would get there eventually, but it would have been a lot longer. So I am glad for what I went through. It opened the doors for a lot of people. (Rodney King)

127. Every time you see a black romance, it's over-the-top. There always has to be extreme hostility between the sexes. He has to cheat. She has to show him how independently strong she is, not just as a woman but as a black woman. (Bernie Mac)

128. "Until it happened, I really did believe that no Black person would ever shoot me. I believed that I didn't have to fear my own community, You know, I was like I represent them. I'm their ambassador to the world, they will never do me wrong." (Tupac Shakur)

129. There's no way I can represent for everyone. I can't represent for all women or all big women or all black women. It's important for people not to make celebrities their source

of who they should be in life. I can't take on the pressure of being perfect. Nobody is. (Queen Latifah)

130. My mother was a woman. A black woman. A single mother. Raising two kids on her own. So she was dark skinned. Had short hair. Got no love from nobody except for a group called the Black Panthers. So that's why she was a Black Panther. (Tupac Shakur)

131. Bill Clinton is like a lot of white politicians. They eat soul food, they party with black women, they play the saxophone, but when it comes to domestic and foreign policy, they make the same decisions that are destructive to African people in this country and throughout the world. (Sister Souljah)

132. A white woman has only one handicap to overcome - that of sex. I have two - both sex and race. ... Colored men have only one - that of race. Colored women are the only group in this country who have two heavy handicaps to overcome, that of race as well as that of sex. (Mary Church Terrell)

133. Today masses of black women in the U.S. refuse to acknowledge that they have much to gain by feminist struggle. They fear feminism. They have stood in place so long that they are afraid to move. They fear change. They fear losing what little they have. (bell hooks)

134. Black women have had to develop a larger vision of our society than perhaps any other group. They have had to un-

derstand white men, white women, and black men. And they have had to understand themselves. When black women win victories, it is a boost for virtually every segment of society. (Angela Davis)

135. I think I'm doing a service to black women by portraying myself as a sex machine. I mean, what's wrong with being a sex machine, darling? Sex is large, sex is life, sex is as large as life, so it appeals to anyone that's living, or rather it should. (Grace Jones)

136. My father was a slave and my people died to build this country and I am going to stay here and have a part of it just like you. (Paul Robeson)

137. I used to think I was ugly. I thought I looked like a camel. A person who doesn't love themselves, they will see anything that pops up on their face. I've seen squirrels, I've seen a bird, and I've seen all kinds of animals on my face. But that is the result of self-hate. I've learned to say: 'You know what? I am a beautiful black woman.' (Mary J Blige)

138. When you're a black woman, you seldom get to do what you just want to do; you always do what you have to do. (Dorothy Height)

139. I decided blacks should not have to experience the difficulties I had faced, so I decided to open a flying school and teach other black women to fly. (Bessie Coleman)

140. The liberal psyche wants to protect minorities, to apolo-

gize for imperialism, colonialism, slavery, and the appalling treatment of black people during the civil rights movement. At the same time, they want to continue to defend the rights of individuals. (Ayaan Hirsi Ali)

141. For Black people, we're one of the only groups of people that for some reason to express love of yourself, in some ways, is misconstrued as a dislike for someone else. (Wynton Marsalis)

142. Only black people in the whole neighborhood, so let's break it down: Me, I'm a decent comedian, I'm a'ight. Mary J. Blige, one of the greatest R&B singers to ever walk the Earth. Jay-Z, one of the greatest rappers to ever live. Eddie Murphy, one of the funniest actors to ever, ever do it. Do you know what the white man that lives next door to me does for a living? He's a f*****g dentist. (Chris Rock)

143. We're going to have to debunk the myth that Africa is a heaven for black people -- especially black women. We've been the mule of the world there and the mule of the world here. (Alice Walker)

144. Two parents can't raise a child any more than one. You need a whole community - everybody - to raise a child. And the little nuclear family is a paradigm that just doesn't work. It doesn't work for white people or for black people. Why are we hanging onto it, I don't know. It isolates people into little units - people need a larger unit. (Toni Morrison)

145. The black church often has reinforced certain self images that are damaging to black peoples' beauty, black peoples' confidence. (Cornel West)

146. I don't see black people as victims even though we are exploited. Victims are flat, one- dimensional characters, someone rolled over by a steamroller so you have a cardboard person. We are far more resilient and more rounded than that. I will go on showing there's more to us than our being victimized. Victims are dead. (Kristin Hunter)

147. I believe all Americans who believe in freedom, tolerance and human rights have a responsibility to oppose bigotry and prejudice based on sexual orientation. (Coretta Scott King)

148. My concern was first, for the black people of Mississippi, then I became concerned for black people nationwide, now my concern is for black people all over the world. I began to realize that it's not as much about race as we think it is. It's about the rich vs. the poor. I feel as if the different races are pitted against one another so we won't see the bigger (financial disparity) problem. (David Banner)

149. I don't want the Obama era to be more about symbolism than substance when it comes to black people. I love him, but I love black people even more. (Tavis Smiley)

150. I'm very disappointed in Barack Obama. I was very much in support of him in the beginning, but I cannot support war. I cannot support droning. I cannot support capitulating

to the banks. I cannot support his caving in to Benjamin Netanyahu. I think many black people support him because they're so happy to have handsome black man in the White House. But it doesn't make me happy if that handsome black man in the White House is betraying all of our traditional values of peace, peoplehood, caring about strangers, feeding the hungry, and not bombing children. (Alice Walker)

151. Yes, you can have art films about the triumph of the human spirit and all of that, but you'll have it done with a big-budget icon with a $20 million salary. You'll have Julia Roberts, you'll have Robert Redford, you'll have Russell Crowe doing those films, because if they're going to cost $90 million, they're going to make that movie for a public that's very large and mainstream. They're not going to make it for three or four million black people. (Pam Grier)

152. I have just as much right to stay in America - in fact, the black people have contributed more to America than any other race, because our kids have fought here for what was called "democracy"; our mothers and fathers were sold and bought here for a price. So all I can say when they say "go back to Africa," I say "when you send the Chinese back to China, the Italians back to Italy, etc., and you get on that Mayflower from whence you came, and give the Indians their land back, who really would be here at home?" (Fannie Lou Hammer)

153. The United States has been called the melting pot of the world. But it seems to me that the colored man either missed getting into the pot or he got melted down. (Thurgood Marshall)

154. I say if black people don't unite and begin to support themselves, their communities and their families, they might as well begin to go out of business as a people. Nobody's going to have any mercy. And nobody's going to have any compunction about making slaves out of them. (John Henrik Clarke)

155. Being satisfied to drink the dregs from the cup of human progress will not demonstrate our fitness as a people to exist alongside of others, but when of our own initiative we strike out to build industries, governments, and ultimately empires, then and only then will we as a race prove to our creator and to man in general that we are fit to survive and capable of shaping our own destiny. (Marcus Garvey)

156. So what you do [under apartheid system] is you convince black people that the reason they are being oppressed is because there are some within their community who just can't behave. And if only they could behave, then everyone else would have more freedoms and liberties, which, of course, is not true. (Trevor Noah)

157. Music played a large role in the survival of the black people in America — that and a sense of humor that just couldn't

be enslaved. (Redd Foxx)

158. If Id lived prior to the 1980s, it would have been different, because I would have been playing to prove African Americans are equal. Now, I dont necessarily feel I have to play for black people, because obviously theyre doing everything in all sports. If I can go out there and play for myself and not feel I have to stand for something other than what I want to do, thats good. (Venus Williams)

159. They don't let many black people in the governor's mansion in Alabama, unless they're cleaning. (Charles Barkley)

160. I don't believe in aliens. I don't think aliens or ghosts like black people. We never get abducted; our houses never get haunted. It always happens in rural areas, where no ethnic people live. The day I see somebody from South Central Los Angeles say, 'Man, I got abducted yesterday,' then I'll believe it. (Xzibit)

161. Imagine a film such as Inception with an entire cast of black people – do you think it would be successful? Would people watch it? But no one questions the fact that everyone's white. That's what we have to change (Idris Elba)

162. IQ tests are routinely used as weapons against Black people in particular and minority groups and poor people generally. The tests are based on white middle-class standards, and when we score low on them, the results are used to justify the prejudice that we are inferior and unintelligent.

Since we are taught to believe that the tests are infallible, they have become a self-fulfilling prophecy that cuts off our initiative and brainwashes us. (Huey Newton)

163. As far as I was concerned, the Panthers were 'baaaaaad.' The Party was more than bad; it was bodacious. The sheer audacity of walking onto the California Senate floor with rifles, demanding that Black people have the right to bear arms and the right to self-defense, made me sit back and take a long look at them. (Assata Shakur)

164. Traveling in the segregated South for black people was humiliating. The very fact that there were separate facilities was to say to black people and white people that blacks were so subhuman and so inferior that we could not even use public facilities that white people used. (Diane Nash)

165. If black people mistrust white people, they are mistrusting racism, and that is appropriate. (Jasmine Guy)

166. I maintain that every civil rights bill in this country was passed for white people, not for black people. (Stokely Carmichael)

167. Any black person who clings to the misguided notion that white people represent the embodiment of all that is evil and black people all that is good remains wedded to the very logic of Western metaphysical dualism that is the heart of racist binary thinking. Such thinking is not liberatory. Like the racist educational ideology it mirrors and imitates, it

invites a closing of the mind. (bell hooks)

168. In this country American means white. Everybody else has to hyphenate. (Toni Morrison)

169. Black people lived right by the railroad tracks, and the train would shake their houses at night. I would hear it as a boy, and I thought: I'm gonna make a song that sounds like that. (Little Richard)

170. When I was a kid, no one would believe anything positive that you could say about black people. That's a terrible burden. (Kareem Abdul-Jabbar)

171. While it has become "cool" for white folks to hang out with black people and express pleasure in black culture, most white people do not feel that this pleasure should be linked to unlearning racism. (bell hooks)

172. Black history isn't a separate history. This is all of our history, this is American history, and we need to understand that. It has such an impact on kids and their values and how they view black people. (Karyn Parsons)

173. I was asked for years about being a Republican, probably because most black people are Democrats. My mother heard it once and called me and said 'Charles, Republicans are for the rich people.' And I said, 'Mom, I'm rich.' (Charles Barkley)

174. White Americans today don't know what in the world to do because when they put us behind them, that's where

they made their mistake... they put us behind them, and we watched every move they made. (Fannie Lou Hammer)

175. I remember back in the day when Chuck D called hip-hop the 'black people's CNN.' Well now, hip-hop is more like Fox News. It's biased, and highly suspect. (Saul Williams)

176. Racism is when you have laws set up, systematically put in a way to keep people from advancing, to stop the advancement of a people. Black people have never had the power to enforce racism, and so this is something that white America is going to have to work out themselves. If they decide they want to stop it, curtail it, or to do the right thing... then it will be done, but not until then. (Spike Lee)

177. Daily the Negro is coming more and more to look upon law and justice, not as protecting safeguards, but as sources of humiliation and oppression. The laws are made by men who have little interest in him; they are executed by men who have absolutely no motive for treating the black people with courtesy or consideration; and, finally, the accused law-breaker is tried, not by his peers, but too often by men who would rather punish ten innocent Negroes than let one guilty one escape. (W. E. B. Du Bois)

178. When I'm asked about the relevance to Black people of what I do, I take that as an affront. It presupposes that Black people have never been involved in exploring the heavens, but this is not so. Ancient African empires - Mali, Songhai,

Egypt - had scientists, astronomers. The fact is that space and its resources belong to all of us, not to any one group. (Mae Jemison)

179. It's just like when you've got some coffee that's too black, which means it's too strong. What do you do? You integrate it with cream, you make it weak. But if you pour too much cream in it, you won't even know you ever had coffee. It used to be hot, it becomes cool. It used to be strong, it becomes weak. It used to wake you up, now it puts you to sleep. (Malcolm X)

180. I carry a knife now because I read in a white magazine that all black people carry knives. So I rushed out and bought me one. (Redd Foxx)

181. The acceptance of the facts of African-American history and the African-American historian as a legitimate part of the academic community did not come easily. Slavery ended and left its false images of black people intact. (John Henrik Clarke)

182. My grandmother's grandparents were slaves. My grandmother Big Mama would tell me about the stories she heard as a child growing up in the shadows of a North Carolina plantation. It's only been in my lifetime that blacks have had the right to vote, live in certain areas or hold certain jobs. It is with this black history that I write about the financial challenges African-Americans still have. (Michelle Singletary)

183. Black people in America have come from slavery to other forms of being oppressed and there are some things that come with that - some pain and anger that come with that and we as black people have to deal with it to heal that. White people have to understand it and have some compassion toward it. (Common)

184. The internal sexism within womanhood is very predominant in Hollywood, because we all want to be successful. There's a plug to it: You all have to be skinny! You all have to be pretty! You all have to be likable, because that's the formula that works. On an executive level. On a power level. And it's not always the same working with black people, because of the internalized racism. The colorism. (Viola Davis)

185. God created black people and black people created style. (George C Wolfe)

186. I grew up in the midst of poverty but every black kid that I knew could read and write. We have to talk about the fact that we cannot educate for critical consciousness if we have a group of people who cannot access Fanon, Cabral, or Audre Lorde because they can't read or write. How did Malcolm X radicalize his consciousness? He did it through books. If you deprive working-class and poor black people of access to reading and writing, you are making them that much farther removed from being a class that can engage in revolutionary

resistance. (bell hooks)

187. We as Black people have to tell our own stories. We have to document our history. When we allow someone else to document our history the history becomes twisted and we get written out. We get our noses blown off. (Erykah Badu)

188. Arguably the most important parallel between mass incarceration and Jim Crow is that both have served to define the meaning and significance of race in America. Indeed, a primary function of any racial caste system is to define the meaning of race in its time. Slavery defined what it meant to be black (a slave), and Jim Crow defined what it meant to be black (a second-class citizen). Today mass incarceration defines the meaning of blackness in America: black people, especially black men, are criminals. That is what it means to be black. (Michelle Alexander)

189. We treat racism in this country like it's a style that America went through. Like flared legs and lava lamps. Oh, that crazy thing we did. We were hanging black people. We treat it like a fad instead of a disease that eradicates millions of people. You've got to get it at a lab, and study it, and see its origins, and see what it's immune to and what breaks it down. (Chris Rock)

190. There are some groups that for years and years have not gotten the rights that the majority of human beings have, and it's important to continue to draw these parallels so that when

we think about our future we can change some of the lives of people who love differently than we do, look different than we do, who come from a different class. It's all about bringing awareness to how important it is to be accepting of people, and there will be oppression if one group thinks they're more important or superior. (Janelle Monae)

191. I was told by the general manager that a white player had received a higher raise than me. Because white people required more money to live than black people. That is why I wasn't going to get a raise. (Curt Flood)

192. I think the rich are too rich and the poor are too poor. I don't think the black people are going to rise at all; I think most of them are going to die. (Nina Simone)

193. What would America be like if we loved black people as much as we loved black culture? (Amandla Stenberg)

194. At this time I'd like to say a few words especially to my sisters: SISTERS. BLACK PEOPLE WILL NEVER BE FREE UNLESS BLACK WOMEN PARTICIPATE IN EVERY ASPECT OF OUR STRUGGLE, ON EVERY LEVEL OF OUR STRUGGLE. (Assata Shakur)

195. It's time for Black people to stop playing the separating game of geography, of where the slave ship put us down. We must concentrate on where the slave ship picked us up. (John Henrik Clarke)

196. Black people are the magical faces at the bottom of

society's well. Even the poorest whites, those who must live their lives only a few levels above, gain their self-esteem by gazing down on us. Surely, they must know that their deliverance depends on letting down their ropes. Only by working together is escape possible. Over time, many reach out, but most simply watch, mesmerized into maintaining their unspoken commitment to keeping us where we are, at whatever cost to them or to us. (Derrick Bell)

197. When we talk about race relations in America or racial progress, it's all nonsense. There are no race relations. White people were crazy. Now they're not as crazy. To say that black people have made progress would be to say they deserve what happened to them before…So, to say Obama is progress is saying that he's the first black person that is qualified to be president. That's not black progress. That's white progress. There's been black people qualified to be president for hundreds of years. If you saw Tina Turner and Ike having a lovely breakfast over there, would you say their relationship's improved? Some people would. But a smart person would go, "Oh, he stopped punching her in the face." It's not up to her. Ike and Tina Turner's relationship has nothing to do with Tina Turner. Nothing. It just doesn't. The question is, you know, my kids are smart, educated, beautiful, polite children. There have been smart, educated, beautiful, polite black children for hundreds of years. The advantage that my children

have is that my children are encountering the nicest white people that America has ever produced. Let's hope America keeps producing nicer white people. (Chris Rock)

198. Our people have lost their way. The new moral crusade should be dedicated to bridging the class divide that has emerged within the African American community. We now have two self-perpetuating classes: my friends' kids . . . and a whole lot of others, who haven't had educational opportunities, haven't benefited from affirmative action. We have the largest black middle class in our history, but the percentage of black children living at or beneath the poverty line is very similar to that on the day Dr. King was so brutally assassinated. Excuse me? If King came back he would die all over again. First we have to recognize that the cause of poverty is both structural and behavioral. And the first thing about the behavior part is that we need a moral revolution within the African American community. Look—no white racist makes you get pregnant when you are a black teenager. Look at black immigrants landing here in Boston from Haiti who can't even speak English! After ten years, they own taxi medallions. So it's not simply a matter of racism. I mean these people are as black as anybody, but they have an immigrant mentality. We need to instill an immigrant mentality back into the African American community. Really, the values under which my generation was raised in the '50s were

immigrant values even though we weren't immigrants. The greatest thing you could be was a college-educated Negro. My daddy would say right now if we called him on the phone, "You have to be 10 times smarter than the white boy." He didn't say, "Woe is me!" or "The white man is the devil!" He said, "You can make it, but you have to be 10 times better and show up ready to work." If we could do that in the '50s, four years before Brown v. Board of Education, for goodness sake, and if the Haitians and other West Indians can do it, then we can do it too. It has nothing to do with race. Yes, there's racism out there, but losing these values has been much worse. I'm not sympathetic to anybody who talks endlessly about how we are victims. I think we start with education and with the black equivalent of Hebrew schools. Now, my Jewish friends say that Hebrew schools are the worst institution ever created. But when they have children they send them to Hebrew school. Without Hebrew school there wouldn't be a Jewish people. (Henry Louis Gates being interviewed by Adam Hochschild in *35 Million Ways to Be Black*)

199. Black History Month is in the shortest month of the year, and the coldest-just in case we want to have a parade. (Chris Rock)

200. You go to school, you study about the Germans and the French, but not about your own race. I hope the time will come when you study black history too. (Booker T Washing-

ton)

201. When I was six, God was a white man with a big beard riding on a white cloud. That's the image television pumps. (Ice Cube)

202. I think that the response to the OJ Simpson trial was based on a kind of sensibility that emerged out of the many campaigns to defend black communities against police violence. (Angela Davis)

203. There's some homophobia within black community, but there's some strong homophobia throughout the whole of American society as well, particularly throughout the South to a degree, whether white or black. And since many of us migrated from the South, that could be a strong connection along those lines. (Otis Moss III)

204. Light-skinned black people are seen to be closer to white people. The allegiance to lighter-skinned people has operated in a very destructive way that we have internalized ourselves inside black communities. You look at many of the prominent black people in this society who have been able to do well. Many have been lighter-skinned. (Michael Eric Dyson)

205. The Black skin is not a badge of shame, but rather a glorious symbol of national greatness. (Marcus Garvey)

206. Black culture is a fight. We want to hold on to what we are, but sometimes the things that we are can be totally negative. You have to think: can't we try something new and not

be seen as suspect? (Danny Glover)

207. I adore my black skin and my kinky hair. The Negro hair is more educated than the white man's hair. Because with Negro hair, where you put it, it stays. It's obedient. The hair of the white, just give one quick movement, and it's out of place. It won't obey. If reincarnation exists I want to come back black. (Carolina Maria De Jesus)

208. In the black community when we think of a couselor or sitting down with a therapist there is that taboo attached to people of being psychotic and crazy. Really it's not it's just sitting down having a conversation. (Gabrielle Dennis)

209. If the churches don't move, much of the community won't move. We've got a situation in which a black church is still a major institution in the black community where 55 percent of the black folk attend and over 75 pass through its doors. (Cornel West)

210. White supremacist ideology is based first and foremost on the degradation of black bodies in order to control them. One of the best ways to instill fear in people is to terrorize them. Yet this fear is best sustained by convincing them that their bodies are ugly, their intellect is inherently underdeveloped, their culture is less civilized, and their future warrants less concern than that of other peoples. (Cornell West)

211. Homosexuality in hip-hop is an extension of homosexuality in the black community. The black community is very,

very conservative when it comes to homosexuality, and I don't mean conservative in the good way, like we're saving money. I mean very intolerant. (Talib Kweli)

212. Seven out of 10 black faces you see on television are athletes. The black athlete carries the image of the black community. He carries the cross, in a way, until blacks make inroads in other dimensions. (Arthur Ashe)

213. You never want to be the whitest-sounding black guy in a room. (Jordan Peele)

214. I always tell my students that Malcolm X came both to his spirituality and to his consciousness as a thinker when he had solitude to read. Unfortunately, tragically, like so many young black males, that solitude only came in prison. (bell hooks)

215. With the black male as a teenager, where you're coming from the ghettos and that kind of stuff, you've got to assert yourself, be macho, not let anybody walk over you, so that's where all this unnecessary bullshit comes from - from egos. That's why there are a lot of fights. That's how come the whole thing with rap has been violent. It's because of the male ego. (Q Tip)

216. One of the burdens of being a black male is carrying the heavy weight of other people's suspicions. (Jonathan Capehart)

217. I am a black male who grew up in the inner city of

Atlanta and no one ever followed me in a mall. I don't recall any doors clicking when I crossed the street. And I never had anyone clutching their handbag when I got on an elevator. I guess having two awesome parents who taught me to be a respectful young man paid dividends. (Allen West)

218. Communism forgets that life is individual. Capitalism forgets that life is social, and the kingdom of brotherhood is found neither in the thesis of communism nor the antithesis of capitalism but in a higher synthesis. It is found in a higher synthesis that combines the truths of both. (Martin Luther King Jr)

219. Jails and prisons are designed to break human beings, to convert the population into specimens in a zoo - obedient to our keepers, but dangerous to each other. (Angela Davis)

220. And, for example, like, when you're having the conversation with your child about getting their driver's license. Well, a white family - their biggest fear is just that you're driving safely and that they're minding the rules of the road, whereas a black family - their biggest fear is that their child is going to get pulled over and treated unfairly for a reason that they won't understand. (Regina King)

221. I was the fifth child in a family of six, five boys and one girl. Bless that poor girl. We were very poor; it was the 30s. We survived off of the food and the little work that my father could get working on the roads or whatever the WPA pro-

vided. We were always in line to get food. The survival of our family really depended on the survival of the other black families in that community. We had that village aspect about us, that African sense about us. We always shared what we had with each other. We were able to make it because there was really a total family, a village. (Cecil Williams)

222. There are black men who are madly in love with white women. God bless them, if that's what works for them. I just hope that we can strike a balance that portrays black folks and the black family in a light that's not extreme. Those are the types of characters that I find myself attracted to. (Nia Long)

223. Slavery didnt break up the black families as much as liberal welfare rules. (Andrew Young)

224. If we accept and acquiesce in the face of discrimination, we accept the responsibility ourselves. We should, therefore, protest openly everything ... that smacks of discrimination or slander. (Mary McLeod Bethune)

225. We felt it necessary being the fact that the Olympic Games, for the first time ever [in 1968], had been televised worldwide. The second thing is the fact that it was in Technicolor. Never had the games been shown in color before.We wanted it to be understood that we were representing America, but we were representing Black America in particular, so that's why we put the black glove on. (John Carlos)

226. I'm a good son, a good father, a good husband - I've been married to the same woman for 30 years. I'm a good friend. I finished college, I have my education, I donate money anonymously. So when people criticize the kind of characters that I play on screen, I go, 'You know, that's part of history.' (Samuel L. Jackson)

227. What we need is not a history of selected races or nations, but the history of the world void of national bias, race hate, and religious prejudice. (Carter G Woodson)

228. When I was in the second grade, one of my teachers said, "Where are you going to find a husband? How are you going to find someone darker than you?" I was mortified. I remember seeing a commercial where a woman goes for an interview and doesn't get the job. Then she puts a cream on her face to lighten her skin, and she gets the job! This is the message: that dark skin is unacceptable. I definitely wasn't hearing this from my immediate family - my mother never said anything to that effect - but the voices from the television are usually much louder than the voices of your parents. (Lupita Nyong'o)

229. You may shoot me with your words, you may cut me with your eyes, you may kill me with your hatefulness, but still, like air, I'll rise! (Maya Angelou)

230. Hip-hop is very diverse, but if you only focus on one aspect of it, then what you get is this image of Black America

that is completely contrary to what actually goes on. (Prince)

231. The Black church is extremely important in Black America. I think most Americans themselves believe in a divine power, in a god, and I'm sure that that number increases with Black people. (Harry Lennix)

232. Sitting at the table doesn't make you a diner. You must be eating some of what's on that plate. Being here in America doesn't make you an American. Being born here in America doesn't make you an American. (Malcolm X)

233. It is easier to build strong children than to repair broken men. (Frederick Douglass)

234. Historically it has been a touchy subject, especially in the south where I am from, people don't really talk about it. If they do talk about it, it is often talked about negatively. Nowadays in light of the Black Lives Matter movement I think people should pay attention to these lives also. I think the Black community will really embrace the film [*Moonlight*]. It is about us. It is real. (Andre Holland on homosexuality in the black community)

235. If women were once permitted to read Sophocles and work with logarithms, or to nibble at any side of the apple of knowledge, there would be an end forever to their sewing on buttons and embroidering slippers. (Anna Julia Cooper)

236. I am of the generation of segregation. Black Lives Matter is post. I said today, and I will say all the time, "If Nina [Sim-

one] were here, she'd have her Black Lives Matter [T-shirt] on." I think they're great kids. They don't need me or anybody else to tell them what to do. (Nikki Giovanni)

237. In all of us there is a hunger, marrow-deep, to know our heritage- to know who we are and where we have come from. Without this enriching knowledge, there is a hollow yearning. No matter what our attainments in life, there is still a vacuum, an emptiness, and the most disquieting loneliness. (Alex Haley)

238. Liberty is meaningless where the right to utter one's thoughts and opinions has ceased to exist. That, of all rights, is the dread of tyrants. It is the right which they first of all strike down. They know its power. Thrones, dominions, principalities, and powers, founded in injustice and wrong, are sure to tremble, if men are allowed to reason... Equally clear is the right to hear. To suppress free speech is a double wrong. It violates the rights of the hearer as well as those of the speaker. (Frederick Douglass)

239. I love the pure, peaceable, and impartial Christianity of Christ; I therefore hatethe corrupt, slaveholding, women-whipping, cradle-plundering, partial, and hypocritical Christianity of this land. Indeed, I can see no reason, but the most deceitful one, for calling the religion of this land Christianity. I look upon it as the climax of all misnomers, the boldest of all frauds, and the grossest of all libels. (Frederick

Douglass)

240. I'm not interested in anybody's guilt. Guilt is a luxury that we can no longer afford. I know you didn't do it, and I didn't do it either, but I am responsible for it because I am a man and a citizen of this country and you are responsible for it, too, for the very same reason... Anyone who is trying to be conscious must begin to dismiss the vocabulary which we've used so long to cover it up, to lie about the way things are. (James Baldwin)

241. I love America more than any other country in this world, and, exactly for this reason, I insist on the right to criticize her perpetually. (James Baldwin)

242. It took many years of vomiting up all the filth I'd been taught about myself, and half-believed, before I was able to walk on the earth as though I had a right to be here. (James Baldwin)

243. To be black and conscious in America is to be in a constant state of rage. (James Baldwin)

244. A liberal: someone who thinks he knows more about your experience than you do. (James Baldwin)

245. What passes for identity in America is a series of myths about one's heroic ancestors. It's astounding to me, for example, that so many people really seem to believe that the country was founded by a band of heroes who wanted to be free. (James Baldwin)

246. It is dangerous to be an American Negro male. America has never wanted its Negroes to be men, and does not, generally, treat them as men. It treats them as mascots, pets, or things. (James Baldwin)

247. As a writer, you get to bring attention to something without preaching. I don't believe in being didactic. So if you dramatize something, you automatically bring attention to it if people read it. (Terry McMillan)

248. I'm convinced that we Black women possess a special indestructible strength that allows us to not only get down, but to get up, to get through, and to get over. (Janet Jackson)

249. It appears that my worst fears have been realised: we have made progress in everything yet nothing has changed. (Derek Bell)

250. One day I realized I was living in a country where I was afraid to be black. It was only a country for white people. Not black. So I left. I had been suffocating in the United States... A lot of us left, not because we wanted to leave, but because we couldn't stand it anymore... I felt liberated in Paris. (Josephine Baker)

251. The Negro has been here in America since 1619, a total of 344 years. He is not going anywhere else; this country is his home. He wants to do his part to help make his city, state, and nation a better place for everyone, regardless of color and race. (Medgar Evers)

252. I'm looking to be shot any time I step out of my car... If I die, it will be in a good cause. I've been fighting for America just as much as the soldiers in Vietnam. (Medgar Evers)

253. It may sound funny, but I love the South. I don't choose to live anywhere else. There's land here, where a man can raise cattle, and I'm going to do it some day. There are lakes where a man can sink a hook and fight the bass. There is room here for my children to play and grow, and become good citizens-if the white man will let them.... (Medgar Evers)

254. When a black Jacksonian looks about his home community, he sees a city of over 150,000, of which 40% is Negro, in which there is not a single Negro policeman or policewoman, school crossing guard, or fireman. (Medgar Evers)

255. I think, though, as African-American women, we are always trained to value our community even at the expense of ourselves, and so we attempt to protect the African-American community. (Anita Hill)

256. There were times when I asked myself whether I was being principled or simply a coward.... I was wrapped in the cocoon of tennis early in life, mainly by blacks like my most powerful mentor, Dr. Robert Walter Johnson of Lynchburg, Virginia. They insisted that I be unfailingly polite on the court, unfalteringly calm and detached, so that whites could never accuse me of meanness. I learned well. I look at pho-

tographs of the skinny, frail, little black boy that I was in the early 1950s, and I see that I was my tennis racquet and my tennis racquet was me. It was my rod and my staff. (Arthur Ashe)

257. I was a black boy at the height of the crack era, which meant that my instructors pitched education as the border between those who would prosper in America, and those who would be fed to the great hydra of prison, teenage pregnancy and murder. (TaNehisi Coates)

258. My mom is Jamaican and Chinese, and my dad is Polish and African American, so I'm pretty mixed. My nickname in high school was United Nations. I was fine with it, even though I identify as a black woman. People don't realize it hurts my feelings when someone looks at my hair or my eyes, and says, "But you're not actually black. You're black, but you're not black black, because your eyes are green." I'm like, "What? No, no, I'm definitely black." Even some of my closest friends have said that. It's been a bit touchy for me. (Ayesha Curry)

259. All the girls in the industry are really all about making different the norm. Everyone really wants that to stop being a movement and start being normal. It shouldn't be a movement when someone casts a bunch of black girls, or a girl who isn't the typical size, or someone with freckles. It should be an everyday thing. (Chantelle Brown-Young)

260. I do remember being teased by my cousins on my mom's side for not being black enough. And then I'd spend the summer with my dad and be sent to all white summer camps where I was 'that black girl.' (Lauren London)

261. We have avoided in recent years talking openly and honestly about race out of fear that it will alienate and polarize. In my own view, it's our refusal to deal openly and honestly with race that leads us to keep repeating these cycles of exclusion and division, and rebirthing a caste-like system that we claim we've left behind. (Michelle Alexander)

262. Look at the coded language the Right is using against President Barack Obama. Openly calling him a liar in Congress, saying he is 'not a Christian, he was not born here, he is not one of us.' That makes addressing such issues trickier for the first African-American in the White House. (Jesse Jackson)

263. I learned a history not then written in books but one passed from generation to generation on the steps of moonlit porches and beside dying fires in one-room houses, a history of great-grandparents and of slavery and of the days following slavery; of those who lived still not free, yet who would not let their spirits be enslaved. (Mildred D. Taylor)

264. You can pray until you faint, but unless you get up and try to do something, God is not going to put it in your lap. (Fannie Lou Hamer)

265. ... continual hard labor deadens the energies of the soul, and benumbs the faculties of the mind; the ideas become confined, the mind barren, and, like the scorching sands of Arabia, produces nothing; or, like the uncultivated soil, brings forth thorns and thistles. Again, continual hard labor irritates our tempers and sours our dispositions; the whole system become worn out with toil and fatigue; nature herself becomes almost exhausted, and we care but little whether we live or die. (Maria W. Stewart)

266. Christianity is being concerned about [others], not building a million-dollar church while people are starving right around the corner. Christ was a revolutionary person, out there where it was happening. That's what God is all about, and that's where I get my strength. (Fannie Lou Hamer)

267. Whether you have a Ph.D., or no D, we're in this bag together. And whether you're from Morehouse or Nohouse, we're still in this bag together. Not to fight to try to liberate ourselves from the men - this is another trick to get us fighting among ourselves - but to work together with the black man, then we will have a better chance to just act as human beings, and to be treated as human beings in our sick society. (Fannie Lou Hamer)

268. I saw in Chicago, on the street where I was visiting my sister-in-law, this "Urban Renewal" and it means one thing: "Negro removal." But they want to tear the homes down

and put a parking lot there. Where are those people going? Where will they go? And as soon as Negroes take to the street demonstrating, one hears people say, "they shouldn't have done it." The world is looking at America and it is really beginning to show up for what it is really like. "Go Tell It on the Mountain." We can no longer ignore this, that America is not "the land of the free and the home of the brave." (Fannie Lou Hamer)

269. And ain't I a woman? Look at me! Look at my arm! I have ploughed and planted, and gathered into barns, and no man could head me! And ain't I a woman? I could work as much and eat as much as a man - when I could get it - and bear the lash as well! And ain't I a woman? I have borne thirteen children, and seen most all sold off to slavery, and when I cried out with my mother's grief, none but Jesus heard me! And ain't I a woman? (Sojourner Truth)

270. Most leaders spend time trying to get others to think highly of them, when instead they should try to get their people to think more highly of themselves. It's wonderful when the people believe in their leader. It's more wonderful when the leader believes in their people! You can't hold a man down without staying down with him. (Booker T. Washington)

271. Most African Americans, if given a chance, would have chosen to be 'just Americans' ever since the first of us was

brought here to Jamestown colony in 1619, a year before the Mayflower landed. But that choice has never been left up to us. (Clarence Page)

272. Everything starts with writing. I heard Nikki Giovanni and was blown away. I just thought 'wow'; she was writing from a black girl's perspective, and the imagery was so vivid that I started doing spoken word. (Jill Scott)

273. I have low self-esteem and I always have. Guys always cheated on me with women who were European-looking. You know, the long-hair type. Really beautiful women that left me thinking, 'How I can I compete with that?' Being a regular black girl wasn't good enough. (Lil Kim)

274. But at the end of the day, I refuse to believe there arent more qualified African-Americans, women, people of color in general for a role from the janitor all the way up to the owner of the club. I refuse to believe there arent more out there that can positively affect any of our games or any of our industries. (Tony Clark)

275. All my friends were in the park smoking weed and getting pregnant. I didn't want to be the young black girl having a baby, a baby's father, being on welfare. That wasn't going to be my story. (Foxy Brown)

276. I am not tragically colored. There is no great sorrow dammed up in my soul, nor lurking behind my eyes. I do not mind at all. I do not belong to the sobbing school of Negro-

hood who hold that nature somehow has given them a low-down dirty deal and whose feelings are all hurt about it. Even in the helter-skelter skirmish that is my life, I have seen that the world is to the strong regardless of a little pigmentation more or less. No, I do not weep at the world—I am too busy sharpening my oyster knife. (Zora Neale Hurston)

277. People ask me if I miss the States. I miss African Americans. But not the U.S. government or all the things they put me through. I miss African American culture, our speech, dance and cooking. (Assata Shakur)

278. My mother always told me to embrace both sides of my background. And she also taught me one very useful thing when I was going to first grade. She said, "You're Bahamian and African-American on one side, and Russian-Jewish on the other. You're no more one than the other, and it's beautiful that you have all this. It makes your life all the more rich. But society will see you only as black." (Lenny Kravitz)

279. If you come to me and say, 'Hey look I'm a racist,' or 'I discriminate against blacks,' or 'I don't like you because you're African American,' I respect that. I can respect you more by doing that. But don't smile in my face, shake my hand, and then you don't really respect me, or want me to be around, or come to your games as the owner of the Clippers. (Magic Johnson)

280. I do not pray. . . . I do not expect God to single me out

and grant me advantages over my fellow men. . . . Prayer seems to me a cry of weakness, and an attempt to avoid, by trickery, the rules of the game as laid down. I do not choose to admit weakness. I accept the challenge of responsibility. (Zora Neale Hurston)

281. Very few Black people ever embraced back to Africa movements, and very few actually, a tiny number actually went back to Africa. They said, "We are going to make America live up to the ideals of the Declaration of Independence and the Constitution of the United States." They produced one of the world's great cultures; they produced individuals who were just as brilliant and made contributions to the world civilization. In fact, they produced a world-class civilization, the African American civilization, in music, in dance, in oratory, in religion, in writing. (Henry Louis Gates)

282. As an African American child growing up in the segregated South, I was told, one way or another, almost every day of my life, that I wasn't as good as a white child. (Coretta Scott King)

283. We've had now eight years and there's this prideful sense among many African Americans. When you think about how elated they are when they see the First Lady on magazine covers or when she is out doing her thing. There just this pride our community has had for eight years now. When that goes away, I jokingly said it, but I do think there's going to be

a bit of withdrawal. (Ed Gordon)

284. When you have a policy of making sure that African Americans cannot build wealth, of plundering African American communities of wealth, giving opportunities to other people, it's only right that you might want to, you know, pay that back. (Ta-Nehisi Coates)

285. What is the alt-right? It's a dressed-up term for white nationalism. They call themselves white identitarianism. They say that the tribalism that's inherent in the human spirit ought to be also applied to white people. (Joy-Ann Reid)

286. I do think that we have to be careful not to assume that getting a perm or wearing a blonde wig is a desire for whiteness. It may or may not be. Listen, I live in a poor black neighborhood where women wear blue hair, green hair, and all kinds of stuff. So, I simply see it as a different set of choices. (Melissa Harris Perry)

287. So, for y'all that can sit around and say all lives matter, I want you to go, put it on a poster, and stand out on a corner somewhere. If we can get enough white people to show that all lives matter, maybe they'll stop killing our black brothers. Cuz obviously, that's what it's going to take; for the white people to get up and get tired of black people [alone] saying black lives matter. So if y'all want it to stop, you get out there and do something about. (Sandra Bland)

288. "This thing that I'm holding in my hand, this telephone,

this camera. It is quite powerful. Social media is powerful. We can do something with this. If we want a change, we can really, truly make it happen." (Sandra Bland)

289. No nation, savage or civilized, save only the United States of America, has confessed its inability to protect its women save by hanging, shooting, and burning alleged offenders (Ida B. Wells)

290. Please stop using the word "Negro."... We are the only human beings in the world with fifty-seven variety of complexions who are classed together as a single racial unit. Therefore, we are really truly colored people, and that is the only name in the English language which accurately describes us. (Mary Church Terrell)

291. We need to stop playing Privilege or Oppression Olympics because we'll never get anywhere until we find more effective ways of talking through difference. We should be able to say, "This is my truth," and have that truth stand without a hundred clamoring voices shouting, giving the impression that multiple truths cannot coexist. (Roxane Gay)

292. People who are overweight face discrimination. African-Americans face discrimination. Women face discrimination and sexism. So I don't have the luxury of not being tolerant of anyone. (Octavia Spencer)

293. There should be a class on drugs. There should be a class on sex education-a real sex education class-not just pictures

and diaphragms and 'un-logical' terms and things like that..... there should be a class on scams, there should be a class on religious cults, there should be a class on police brutality, there should be a class on apartheid, there should be a class on racism in America, there should be a class on why people are hungry, but there are not, there are classes on gym, physical education, let's learn volleyball. (Tupac Shakur)

294. I find that people today tend to use them interchangeably. I use African-American, because I teach African Studies as well as African-American Studies, so it's easy, neat and convenient. But sometimes, when you're in a barber shop, somebody'll say, "Did you see what that Negro did?" A lot of people slip in and out of different terms effortlessly, and I don't think the thought police should be on patrol. (Henry Louis Gates)

295. We think that if we get tested, that means you have to have HIV. Or we think that just by knowing someone with HIV, we're going to get HIV or because he's gay or she's a lesbian or whatever. This false information has been put out there and it's created this stigma that stops us from going to find out if we're infected. The truth is it doesn't matter who you are, if you're having sex, you need to be getting tested, plain and simple. (Jay Ellis)

296. A woman in the Black Power movement was considered, at best, irrelevant. A woman asserting herself was a pariah.

If a black woman assumed a role of leadership, she was said to be eroding black manhood, to be hindering the progress of the black race. She was an enemy of the black people.... I knew I had to muster something mighty to manage the Black Panther Party. (Elaine Brown)

297. I'm through with you. Yes, I am going to put you down. From now on, I am my own God. I am going to live by the rules I se for myself. I'll discard everything I was once taught about you. Then I'll be you. I'll be my own God, living my life as I see fit. Not as Mr. Charlie says I should live it, or Mama or anybody else. I shall do as I want in this society that apparently wasn't meant for me and my kind. If you are getting angry because I am talking to you like this, then just kill me, leave me here in this graveyard dead. Maybe thats where all of us belong anyway. Maybe then we wouldn't have to suffer so much. At the rate we are being killed now, we'll all be soon dead anyway. (Anne Moody in *Coming of Age in Mississippi*)

298. You know what? I never really factor Hollywood into anything. I'm a black actor, so I can't really control what Hollywood thinks. I gotta go do my thing, and my jokes have got to be funny. Whatever I do has got to be great. (Jamie Foxx)

299. I know that the blacks, take them half enlightened and ignorant, are more humane and merciful than the most enlightened and refined European that can be found in all the earth. (David Walker)

300. Sometimes Mama would bring us the white family's left-overs. It was the best food I had ever eaten. That what when I discovered that white folks ate different from us. They had all kinds of different food with meat and all. We always just had beans and bread. One Saturday the white lady let Mama bring us to her house… The kitchen was pretty, all white and shiny… 'If Mama only had a kitchen like this of her own,' I thought, 'she would cook better food for us." (Anne Moody in *Coming of Age in Mississippi*)

301. People talk about Jim Crow as if it's dead. Jim Crow isn't gone. It's adjusted. Look at the disproportionate sentences meted out to blacks caught up in the criminal justice system. There's a problem when people profit from putting and keeping African Americans in prison. We need to do a better job as a nation understanding the real values the country's built upon in terms of fairness, equality and equal opportunity. (Aldis Hodge)

302. Don't blame Wall Street, don't blame the big banks. If you don't have a job and you are not rich, blame yourself! (Herman Cain)

303. Invest in the human soul. Who knows, it might be a diamond in the rough. (Mary McLeod Bethune)

304. I don't do things for the response or for the controversy. I just live my life. (Rihanna)

305. We must recognize that we can't solve our problem

now until there is a radical redistribution of economic and political power… this means a revolution of values and other things. We must see now that the evils of racism, economic exploitation and militarism are all tied together… you can't really get rid of one without getting rid of the others… the whole structure of American life must be changed. America is a hypocritical nation and [we] must put [our] own house in order. (Martin Luther King Jr. to SCLC Staff, May 1967)

306. Out of frustration and hopelessness our young people have reached the point of no return. We no longer endorse patience and turning the other cheek. We assert the right of self-defense by whatever means necessary, and reserve the right of maximum retaliation against our racist oppressors, no matter what the odds against us are. (Sanyika Shakur in *Monster: The Autobiography of an LA Gang Member*)

307. If America does not use her vast resources of wealth to end poverty and make it possible for all of God's children to have the basic necessities of life, she too will go to hell. (Martin Luther King Jr. , two weeks before he was assassinated.)

308. I came to see through my writing that no matter how hard we in the movement worked, nothing seemed to change. We were like an angry dog on a leash that had turned on its master. It could bark and howl and snap, and sometimes even bite, but the master was always in control. (Anne Moody)

309. My mom experienced racism. She was harassed by the

KKK several times. And I experienced racism myself, growing up. In New Jersey, we had trash thrown on our lawn every day. And we had the lines to our Christmas lights cut three years in a row. We just stopped putting up Christmas lights after that. That's probably why I still don't put up any lights during the holidays. (Aldis Hodge)

310. You can't talk about solving the economic problem of the Negro without talking about billions of dollars. You can't talk about ending the slums without first saying profit must be taken out of slums. You're really tampering and getting on dangerous ground because you are messing with folk then. You are messing with captains of industry. Now this means that we are treading in difficult water, because it really means that we are saying that something is wrong with capitalism. (Martin Luther King Jr.,1966)

311. Herein lies the tragedy of the age: not that men are poor—all men know something of poverty; not that men are wicked—who is good? Not that men are ignorant—what is truth? Nay, but that men know so little of men. (W.E.B. Du Bois)

312. When old people speak it is not because of the sweetness of words in our mouths; it is because we see something which you do not see. (Chinua Achebe)

313. If there is a book that you want to read, but it hasn't been written yet, you must be the one to write it. (Toni Morrison)

314. I never had anything good, no sweet, no sugar; and that sugar, right by me, did look so nice, and my mistress's back was turned to me while she was fighting with her husband, so I just put my fingers in the sugar bowl to take one lump, and maybe she heard me, for she turned and saw me. The next minute, she had the rawhide down. (Harriet Tubman)

315. Plenty of the colored women have children by the white men. She know better than to not do what he say. Didn't have much of that until the men from South Carolina come up here [North Carolina] and settle and bring slaves. Then they take them very same children what have they own blood and make slaves out of them. If the Missus find out she raise revolution. But she hardly find out. The white men not going to tell and the nigger women were always afraid to. So they jes go on hopin' that thing[s] won't be that way always. (W. L. Bost interviewed in 1937's *WPA Slave Narrative Project*)

316. The slave traders would buy young and able farm men and well developed young girls with fine physique to barter and sell. They would bring them to the taverns where there would be the buyers and traders, display them and offer them for sale. At one of these gatherings a colored girl, a mulatto of fine stature and good looks, was put on sale. She was of high spirits and determined disposition. At night she was taken by the trader to his room to satisfy his bestial nature. She could not be coerced or forced, so she was attacked by him. In the

struggle she grabbed a knife and with it, she sterilized him and from the result of injury he died the next day. She was charged with murder. Gen. Butler, hearing of it, sent troops to Charles County [Maryland] to protect her, they brought her to to Baltimore, later she was taken to Washington where she was set free. . . This attack was the result of being good-looking, for which many a poor girl in Charles County paid the price. There are several cases I could mention, but they are distasteful to me. . . .There was a doctor in the neighborhood who bought a girl and installed her on the place for his own use, his wife hearing it severely beat her. One day her little child was playing in the yard. It fell head down in a post hole filled with water and drowned. His wife left him; afterward she said it was an affliction put on her husband for his sins. Let me explain to you very plain without prejudice one way or the other, I have had many opportunities, a chance to watch white men and women in my long career, colored women have many hard battles to fight to protect themselves from assault by employers, white male servants or by white men, many times not being able to protect [themselves], in fear of losing their positions. Then on the other hand they were subjected to many impositions by the women of the household through woman's jealousy. (Richard Macks in 1937's *WPA Slave Narrative Project*)

317. He had so many slaves he did not know all their names.

His fortune was his slaves. He did not sell slaves and he did not buy many, the last ten years preceding the war. He resorted to raising his own slaves. A slave girl was expected to have children as soon as she became a woman. Some of them had children at the age of twelve and thirteen years old. . . Mother said there were cases where these young girls loved someone else and would have to receive the attentions of men of the master's choice. This was a general custom. . . The masters called themselves Christians, went to church worship regularly and yet allowed this condition to exist. Hilliard Yellerday in 1937's *WPA Slave Narrative Project*]

318. I was born in North Carolina, in Caswell County, I am not able to tell in what month or year. What I shall now relate is what was told me by my mother and grandmother. A few months before I was born, my father married my mother's young mistress. As soon as my father's wife heard of my birth, she sent one of my mother's sisters to see whether I was white or black, and when my aunt had seen me, she returned back as soon as she could and told her mistress that I was white and resembled Mr. Roper very much. Mr. Roper's wife not being pleased with this report, she got a large club-stick and knife, and hastened to the place in which my mother was confined. She went into my mother's room with a full intention to murder me with her knife and club, but as she was going to stick the knife into me, my grandmother happening

to come in, caught the knife and saved my life. But as well as I can recollect from what my mother told me, my father sold her and myself soon after her confinement. (Moses Roper, *Narrative of the Adventures and Escape of Moses Roper, from American Slavery*, 1840)

319. There is something akin to freedom in having a lover who has no control over you, except that which he gains by kindness and attachment. (Harriet Ann Jacobs)

320. Love is or it ain't. Thin love ain't love at all. (Toni Morrison)

321. People always say that I didn't give up my seat because I was tired, but that isn't true. I was not tired physically... No, the only tired I was, was tired of giving in. (Rosa Parks)

322. Just because I let her lick my ass, she thinks I'm gay. (50 Cent)

323. I would be really offended if there was a school that was known as a historically white college. We have historically Black colleges. What if there was the National Organization for White People, only? There's the NAACP. (Wendy Williams)

324. I would rather drudge out my life on a cotton plantation, till the grave opened to give me rest, than to live with an unprincipled master and a jealous mistress. (Harriet Jacobs)

325. It always seems impossible until it's done. (Nelson Mandela)

326. If you talk to a man in a language he understands, that goes to his head. If you talk to him in his language, that goes to his heart. (Nelson Mandela)

327. Begging for acknowledgment, or even asking, diminishes dignity and diminishes power. And we are a dignified people, and we are powerful. So let's let the Academy do them, with all grace and love. And let's do us, differently. (Jada Pinkett Smith when boycotting the Oscars in 2016)

328. Just a moment. I'm going to Beyoncé you. Boy, bye. You are just so out of line right now. Tell your candidate to release his tax returns. (Angela Rye on CNN to a Trump supporter)

329. I think absolutely my son's race and the color of his skin had a lot to do with why he was shot and killed, in all of these cases, these victims were unarmed. These victims were African-American. That needs to be our conversation. (Sybrina Fulton, mother of Trayvon Martin)

330. The Trayvon Martin movement was not created to incite hate or further racial divide, but rather birthed to raise awareness to the social injustices that exist across America with regards to senseless gun violence against our young black and brown boys; the movement also focuses on the growing disparities in the lack of prosecution of the actual perpetrators. (Sybrina Fulton)

331. I know that he's been my angel through this all and I know that he's proud of me. (Mike Brown's mother Lesley

McSpadden on getting her high school diploma in honor of her son in May 2017)

332. Because I know that the people are not protected against the police. I wanted to make sure if I died in front of my daughter that people would know the truth. (Diamond Reynolds in June 2017 when explaining why she decided to record the interaction with police that captured the murder of her boyfriend Philando Castille)

333. Some problems we share as women, some we do not. You fear your children will grow up to join the patriarchy and testify against you; we fear our children will be dragged from a car and shot down in the street, and you will turn your backs on the reasons they are dying. (Audre Lorde)

334. Just get a regular word. What the fuck is a Google? (DMX)

335. I'm not saying I'm gonna change the world, but I guarantee that I will spark the brain that will change the world. (Tupac Shakur)

336. How the fuck can I be a Republican when I got a song called 'Fuck tha Police'? (Eazy E defending his 1991 visit to the White House after accidentally being invited)

337. It is a peculiar sensation, this double-consciousness, this sense of always looking at one's self through the eyes of others... One ever feels his twoness,—an American, a Negro; two souls, two thoughts, two unreconciled strivings; two warrings

ideals in one dark body, whose dogged strength alone keeps it from being torn asunder. (W.E.B. Du Bois)

338. Service is the rent we pay for being. It is the very purpose of life, and not something you do in your spare time. (Marian Wright Edelman)

339. If you don't like the way the world is, you change it. You have an obligation to change it. You just do it one step at a time. (Marian Wright Edelman)

340. Why is it that, as a culture, we are more comfortable seeing two men holding guns than holding hands? (Ernest J Gaines)

341. I wasn't really naked. I simply didn't have any clothes on. (Josephine Baker)

342. You must get an education. You must go to school, and you must learn to protect yourself. And you must learn to protect yourself with the pen, and not the gun. (Josephine Baker)

343. A myth is an old lie that people believe in. White people believe that they're better than anyone else on earth - and that's a myth. (Ernest Gaines)

344. The Negro was freed and turned loose as a penniless, landless, naked, ignorant laborer. Ninety-nine per cent were field hands and servants of the lowest class. (W. E. B. Du Bois)

345. I do believe that my whole success goes back to that

time I was arrested as a wayward boy at the age of thirteen. Because then I had to quit running around and began to learn something. Most of all, I began to learn music. (Louis Armstrong)

346. I never cut class. I loved getting A's, I liked being smart. I liked being on time. I thought being smart is cooler than anything in the world. (Michelle Obama)

347. I was married to Bill McDonald in 1960. People would say 'Why didn't you marry a Black man?' I would reply "because the white girls had them!" The men I wanted to be with, Sidney Poitier, Harry Belafonte, dated predominatly white women. I'm talking about the 50s. When Harry Belfonte picks me out of his bed in Philadelphia and said: 'I don't want you to take me seriously because no Black woman can do anything for me'. I could not help him to progress into where he was going to go. "A black woman would hold a black man back', that's what he told me. If I wanted to marry a black man there wasn't one because the white girls had them. (Eartha Kitt)

348. My experiences at Princeton have made me far more aware of my 'blackness' than ever before. I have found that at Princeton, no matter how liberal and open-minded some of my white professors and classmates try to be toward me, I sometimes feel like a visitor on campus; as if I really don't belong. (Michelle Obama)

349. Reconstruction was a vast labor movement of ignorant, muddled, and bewildered white men who had been disinherited of land and labor and fought a long battle with sheer subsistence, hanging on the edge of poverty, eating clay and chasing slaves and now lurching up to manhood. (W. E. B. Du Bois)

350. School houses do not teach themselves - piles of brick and mortar and machinery do not send out men. It is the trained, living human soul, cultivated and strengthened by long study and thought, that breathes the real breath of life into boys and girls and makes them human, whether they be black or white, Greek, Russian or American. (W. E. B. Du Bois)

351. I am a feminist, and what that means to me is much the same as the meaning of the fact that I am Black: it means that I must undertake to love myself and to respect myself as though my very life depends upon self-love and self-respect. (June Jordan)

352. Winning is great, sure, but if you are really going to do something in life, the secret is learning how to lose. Nobody goes undefeated all the time. If you can pick up after a crushing defeat, and go on to win again, you are going to be a champion someday. (Wilma Rudolph)

353. "Whatever you fear most has no power – it is your fear that has the power. The thing itself cannot touch you. But if

you allow your fear to seep into your mind and overtake your thoughts, it will rob you of your life." (Oprah Winfrey)

354. I used to want the words 'She tried' on my tombstone. Now I want 'She did it.'" (Katherine Dunham)

355. I knew that I lived in a country in which the aspirations of black people were limited, marked-off. Yet I felt that I had to go somewhere and do something to redeem my being alive. (Richard Wright)

356. The white folks like for us to be religious, then they can do what they want to with us. (Richard Wright)

357. I'm not a 'Business-Man'! I'm a Business... man! Let me handle my business, damn! (Jay Z)

358. Many African-American boys feel loathed before they are loved, feel rejected before they are respected, and feel alienated before they are educated. These feelings often morph into expressions of anger. (Alfred W Tatum)

359. The burden of poverty isn't just that you don't always have the things you need, it's the feeling of being embarrassed every day of your life, and you'd do anything to lift that burden. (Jay-Z)

360. I'm a mirror. If you're cool with me, I'm cool with you, and the exchange starts. What you see is what you reflect. If you don't like what you see, then you've done something. If I'm standoffish, that's because you are. I'm a mirror. If you're cool with me, I'm cool with you, and the exchange starts.

What you see is what you reflect. If you don't like what you see, then you've done something. If I'm standoffish, that's because you are. (Jay-Z)

361. This is a critical juncture in our history. Many young people of color in economically underdeveloped communities are becoming deeply rooted in personal and academic dormancy that interrupts their ability to invest in our fast-moving, ever-changing, increasingly demanding world." (Alfred W. Tatum in *Reading for Their Life: (Re)Building the Textual Lineages of African American Adolescent Males*)

362. You have to act as if it were possible to radically transform the world. And you have to do it all the time. (Angela Davis)

363. During those long years in Oakland public schools, I did not have one teacher who taught me anything relevant to my own life or experience. Not one instructor ever awoke in me a desire to learn more or to question or to explore the worlds of literature, science, and history. All they did was try to rob me of the sense of my own uniqueness and worth, and in the process nearly killed my urge to inquire. (Huey Newton)

364. Settle your quarrels, come together, understand the reality of our situation, understand that fascism is already here, that people are already dying who could be saved, thatgenerations more will live poor butchered half-lives if you fail to act. Do what must be done, discover your humanity and your

love in Revolution. (George Jackson)

365. I did not have any problem with speaking up because my mother, my family, my grandmother, my aunt - I grew up in a family dominated by women - always encouraged me to do so. And if a girl is unafraid, then the world is her oyster. (Ava DuVernay)

366. How I grew to believe Black hair has power, genius, and magic in it, defying gravity and limitation. I mean, look at how marvelous it is: Black hair grows up and out. (Michaela Angela Davis)

367. Patience has its limits. Take it too far, and it's cowardice. (George Jackson)

368. Today there are more African-Americans under correctional control — in prison or jail, on probation or parole — than were enslaved in 1850, a decade before the Civil War began. There are millions of African-Americans now cycling in and out of prisons and jails or under correctional control. In major American cities today, more than half of working-age African-American men are either under correctional control or branded felons and are thus subject to legalized discrimination for the rest of their lives. (Michelle Alexander)

369. My grandmother and my two aunts were an exhibition in resilience and resourcefulness and black womanhood. They rarely talked about the unfairness of the world with the words that I use now with my social justice friends, words like

"intersectionality" and "equality", "oppression", and "discrimination". They didn't discuss those things because they were too busy living it, navigating it, surviving it." (Janet Mock in *Redefining Realness: My Path to Womanhood, Identity, Love & So Much More*)

370. We have defeated Jim Crow, but now we have to deal with his son, James Crow Jr., esquire. (Al Sharpton)

371. All people make mistakes. All of us are sinners. All of us are criminals. All of us violate the law at some point in our lives. In fact, if the worst thing you have ever done is speed ten miles over the speed limit on the freeway, you have put yourself and others at more risk of harm than someone smoking marijuana in the privacy of his or her living room. Yet there are people in the United States serving life sentences for first-time drug offenses, something virtually unheard of anywhere else in the world. (Michelle Alexander)

372. I'm always telling the brothers some of those whites are willing to work with us against the pigs. All they got to do is stop talking honky. When the races start fighting, all you have is one maniac group against another. (George Jackson)

373. While the rest of the country waves the flag of Americana, we understand we are not part of that. We don't owe America anything - America owes us. (Al Sharpton)

374. Prison is the only form of public housing that the government has truly invested in over the past 5 decades (Marc

Lamont Hill)

375. Nothing lasts forever, whether it's Greece, Rome or the British Empire. It doesn't mean that America has to end. The country could be reshaped and reimagined in a way that is even more democratic and less imperial in nature. We're trying to radically reshape the nation in ways that are more just and fairer. That's what I mean when I say that empires eventually fall. I'm not calling for the end of America. I'm just calling for a reimagination of its democratic possibilities. (Marc Lamont Hill)

376. I'd much rather have AIDS than a baby... They're not that different at all. They're both expensive, you have them for the rest of your life, they're constant reminders of the mistakes you've made and once you have them, you pretty much can only date other people who have them. (Donald Glover)

377. Listen, here's reality. It is completely unfair and absolutely necessary that people who have been oppressed and marginalized have to lead everybody. That is MLK, that is Dolores Huerta, that is Fannie Lou Hamer, that is Ella Jo Baker, that is Nelson Mandela. You walk down the line. (Van Jones)

378. I don't think my films are going to get rid of racism or prejudice. I think the best thing my films can do is provoke discussion. (Spike Lee)

379. In the U.S., African- Americans, no matter what we do - when we sit in, when we freedom ride, when we kneel in,

whatever it is, the initial response from the public tends to be overwhelmingly negative, because basically we're kind of raining on folks' parades. As time goes on, the Muhammad Ali's and all the people that raised those issues, they then become heroes later when people reflect on the courage they showed and the issues that they raised. And Donald Trump is in danger of being a more and more reviled figure as the years go on. (Van Jones)

380. Do you see law and order? There is nothing but disorder, and instead of law there is the illusion of security. It is an illusion because it is built on a long history of injustices: racism, criminality, and the genocide of millions. Many people say it is insane to resist the system, but actually, it is insane not to. (Mumia Abu-Jamal)

381. Poor people of all colors are getting poorer and our communities are getting more toxic. There is a misconception that to grow our economy we will have to do business as usual, because cleaning up the environment, mitigating climate change is just too costly. Well, I say the business of poverty is just too expensive a bill for humanity to pay any longer. (Majora Carter)

382. Race and class are extremely reliable indicators as to where one might find the good stuff, like parks and trees, and where one might find the bad stuff, like power plants and waste facilities. (Majora Carter)

383. At the risk of quoting Mephistopheles I repeat: Welcome to hell. A hell erected and maintained by human-governments, and blessed by black robed judges. A hell that allows you to see your loved ones, but not to touch them. A hell situated in America's boondocks, hundreds of miles away from most families. A white, rural hell, where most of the captives are black and urban. It is an American way of death. (Mumia Abu-Jamal)

384. I think, when you're great, not everyone's going to give you your props, and you can't really worry about that. In my eyes, I'm still climbing. I'm still taking myself to the next levels in my career, and that's fine with me. When it's time for my rewards, I will get them. (Lil' Kim)

385. All my life, men have told me I wasn't pretty enough - even the men I was dating. And I'd be like, 'Well, why are you with me, then?' It's always been men putting me down just like my dad. To this day when someone says I'm cute, I can't see it. I don't see it no matter what anybody says. (Lil' Kim)

386. I really wish Hollywood would stop labeling movies, especially movies with predominantly black casts. Then, it makes others feel like, "Oh, well, that's not for me." At the end of the day, everybody understands love, loss, pain and heartbreak. That's not a color. (Taraji P. Henson)

387. I am not going to stand up to show pride in a flag for a country that oppresses black people and people of color.

(Colin Kaepernick)

388. I realize that men and women of the military go out and sacrifice their lives and put their selves in harm's way for my freedom of speech and my freedoms in this country, and my freedom to take a seat or take a knee, so I have the utmost respect for them, and I think what I did was taken out of context and spun a different way. (Colin Kaepernick)

389. People like rumors. They're going to say things like, 'You was at the club with Lil' Kim, and you and Kanye West got into a fist fight.' You can't get upset. You've got to keep hope alive. (Bernie Mac)

390. You loan your friend money. You see them again, they don't say nothin' 'bout the money. 'Hi, how ya doin'? How's ya mama doing?' Man, how's my money doin'? (Chris Tucker)

391. People say, 'Why is he bored with her?' Because he's a human being, that's why; same way his wife is bored with him. That is marriage - anything that's supposed to be forever, your going to get bored with it. And there is nothing wrong with it, so don't take it personal; if you are with somebody for ten years and they are not bored with you? Then something is wrong with them. (Chris Rock)

392. I feel most people's sexuality is enormously complicated. That's what it means to be human. Wouldn't it be great if we honored that complexity rather than turn it into gossip or ridicule? Wouldn't it be great if we accepted sexual diversi-

ty, in ourselves and others, without condemning it? (Janet Jackson)

393. If you're a black Christian, you have a real short memory. (Chris Rock)

394. First of all, let's get one thing straight. Crack is cheap. I make too much money to ever smoke crack. Let's get that straight. OK? We don't do crack. We don't do that. Crack is whack. (Whitney Houston)

395. "There is nothing in our book, the Koran, that teaches us to suffer peacefully. Our religion teaches us to be intelligent. Be peaceful, be courteous, obey the law, respect everyone; but if someone puts his hand on you, send him to the cemetery. That's a good religion." (Malcolm X)

396. Instead of looking at the past, I put myself ahead twenty years and try to look at what I need to do now in order to get there then. (Diana Ross)

397. I was a victim; I don't dwell on it. (Tina Turner)

398. If I didn't have some kind of education, then I wouldn't be able to count my money. (Missy Elliot)

399. "I am a Muslim and there is nothing Islamic about killing innocent people in Paris, San Bernardino, or anywhere else in the world. True Muslims know that the ruthless violence of so-called Islamic Jihadists goes against the very tenets of our religion." (Muhammad Ali in 2015)

400. When interviewers ask me who I'm sleeping with or if I

don't like such-and-such or what is my sexuality, that's not beneficial to the world. They need to ask me about stuff that may help readers, like how my father abused my mother for many years. A lot of kids go through that and need to know what they should do. (Missy Elliot)

401. Fear can be good when you're walking past an alley at night or when you need to check the locks on your doors before you go to bed, but it's not good when you have a goal and you're fearful of obstacles. We often get trapped by our fears, but anyone who has had success has failed before. (Queen Latifah)

402. I feel money is power in certain senses. A lot of women out there are just givin' it away. And then there are the women that're selling their bodies. But they chose to do that. But this is how they make their money. And I don't see anything wrong with that. (Lil' Kim)

403. I realized that I was African when I came to the United States. Whenever Africa came up in my college classes, everyone turned to me. It didn't matter whether the subject was Namibia or Egypt; I was expected to know, to explain. (Chimamanda Ngozi Adichie)

404. Popular films are so powerful and compelling that it's often easier to accept their versions of history than the much more complicated true stories. (Melissa Harris-Perry)

405. Beauty is not just a white girl. It's so many different fla-

vors and shades. (Queen Latifah)

406. Society has a problem with female nudity when it is not ... when it is not packaged for the consumption of male entertainment. Then it becomes confusing." (Erykah Badu)

407. So close is the bond between man and woman that you can not raise one without lifting the other. The world can not move ahead without woman's sharing in the movement, and to help give a right impetus to that movement is woman's highest privilege. (Frances Ellen Harper)

408. Only the BLACK WOMAN can say 'when and where I enter, in the quiet, undisputed dignity of my womanhood, without violence and without suing or special patronage, then and there the whole Negro race enters with me.' (Anna Julia Cooper)

409. Either America will destroy ignorance or ignorance will destroy the United States. (W. E. B. Du Bois)

410. We must give up the silly idea of folding our hands and waiting on God to do everything for us. If God had intended for that, then he would not have given us a mind. Whatever you want in life, you must make up your mind to do it for yourself. (Marcus Garvey)

411. A race that is solely dependent upon another for economic existence sooner or later dies. As we have in the past been living upon the mercies shown by others, and by the chances obtainable, and have suffered there from, so we will

in the future suffer if an effort is not made now to adjust our own affairs. (Marcus Garvey)

412. Let our girls feel that we expect something more of them than that they merely look pretty and appear well in society. (Anna Julia Cooper)

413. The white man has succeeded in subduing the world by forcing everybody to think his way....The white man's propaganda has made him the master of the world, and all those who have come in contact with it and accepted it have become his slaves. (Marcus Garvey)

414. I really just want to encourage and inspire people to use their freedom in a positive way and in a way that is inspiring to other people. I want to continue to pass down the seeds of change within the world. I think that it can start with just one person. Just like a rumor can get carried on, so can inspiration. (Janelle Monae)

415. Do not remove the kinks from your hair--remove them from your brain. (Marcus Garvey)

416. "Nobody in the world, nobody in history, has ever gotten their freedom by appealing to the moral sense of the people who were oppressing them." (Assata Shakur)

417. There is a certain class of race problem-solvers who don't want the patient to get well, because as long as the disease holds out they have not only an easy means of making a living, but also an easy medium through which to make them-

selves prominent before the public. (Booker T. Washington)

418. The colored people of this country know and understand the white people better than the white people know and understand them. (James Weldon Johnson)

419. I speak for the colored women of the South, because it is there that the millions of blacks in this country have watered the soil with blood and tears, and it is there too that the colored woman of America has made her characteristic history and there her destiny is evolving. (Anna Julia Cooper)

420. I am not afraid of being sued by white businessmen. In fact, I should welcome such a lawsuit. It would do the cause much good. Let us banish fear. We have been in this mental state for three centuries. I am a radical. I am ready to act, if I can find brave men to help me. (Carter G. Woodson)

421. Take us generally as a people, we are neither lazy nor idle; and considering how little we have to excite or stimulate us, I am almost astonished that there are so many industrious and ambitious ones to be found - although I acknowledge, with extreme sorrow, that there are some who never were and never will be serviceable to society. And have you not a similar class among yourselves? (Maria W. Stewart in 1832's *Why Ye Sit There and Die*)

422. One needs both leisure and money to make a successful book. (Frances Harper)

423. Then that little man in black there, he says women can't

have as much rights as men, 'cause Christ wasn't a woman! Where did your Christ come from? Where did Christ come from? From God and a woman! Man had nothing to do with Him. (Sojourner Truth)

424. Let no man of us budge one step, and let slaveholders come to beat us from our country. America is more our country, than it is the whites-we have enriched it with our blood and tears. The greatest riches in all America have arisen from our blood and tears. (David Walker)

425. Education and justice are democracy's only life insurance. (Nannie Helen Burroughs)

426. Being pregnant was very much like falling in love. You are so open. You are so overjoyed. There's no words that can express having a baby growing inside of you so, of course, you want to scream it out and tell everyone. (Beyonce Knowles)

427. The prison-industrial complex, poverty, and the school system has more effect on a young black male in America than Jay-Z does, by far. And that's not a diss to Jay-Z. The crime rate in the black community was high before hip hop. Rapping about it is just a reflection of the life a lot of people are living. (John Legend)

428. Why would you create a movie for black people if you don't understand the history and perspective of the people you are doing it for? You need historical perspective to make

sound decisions. (Tim Reid)

429. Looking at the incarcerated, these are not political criminals. These are people going around stealing Coca-Cola. People getting shot in the back of the head over a piece of pound cake! And then we all run out and are outraged, 'The cops shouldn't have shot him.' What the hell was he doing with the pound cake in his hand? I wanted a piece of pound cake just as bad as anybody else, and I looked at it and I had no money. And something called parenting said, 'If you get caught with it you're going to embarrass your mother.' Not 'You're going to get your butt kicked.' No. 'You're going to embarrass your family.' (Bill Cosby during a 2004 speech at the NAACP Awards)

430. And it's even worse because Bill Cosby has the fucking smuggest old black man public persona that I hate. Pull your pants up, black people, I was on TV in the '80s. I can talk down to you because I had a successful sitcom. Yeah, but you raped women, Bill Cosby. So, brings you down a couple notches. I don't curse on stage. Well, yeah, you're a rapist, so, I'll take you sayin' lots of motherfuckers on Bill Cosby: Himself if you weren't a rapist. … I want to just at least make it weird for you to watch Cosby Show reruns. … I've done this bit on stage, and people don't believe. People think I'm making it up. … That shit is upsetting. If you didn't know about it, trust me. You leave here and google 'Bill Cosby rape.' It's

not funny. That shit has more results than Hannibal Buress. (Hannibal Buress in 2014)

431. "I had just moved to Harlem. It was the first night I was there, and I went for a walk and there was a rally going on. Of course, I had heard about Malcolm before that, but it was mostly the kind of negative things they were running about him in the press then. I felt as if I was hearing the truth. I had never heard anyone speak with such clarity and forcefulness. And he just stimulated me." (A. Peter Bailey)

432. If you are neutral in situations of injustice, you have chosen the side of the oppressor. If an elephant has its foot on the tail of a mouse, and you say that you are neutral, the mouse will not appreciate your neutrality. (Desmond Tutu)

433. "When the Missionaries arrived, the Africans had the land and the Missionaries had the Bible. They taught how to pray with our eyes closed. When we opened them, they had the land and we had the Bible." (Jomo Kenyatta)

434. If I were not African, I wonder whether it would be clear to me that Africa is a place where the people do not need limp gifts of fish but sturdy fishing rods and fair access to the pond. I wonder whether I would realize that while African nations have a failure of leadership, they also have dynamic people with agency and voices. (Chimamanda Ngozi Adichie)

435. People get used to anything. The less you think about

your oppression, the more your tolerance for it grows. After a while, people just think oppression is the normal state of things. But to become free, you have to be acutely aware of being a slave. (Assata Shakur)

436. I think if we are actually going to accept our generation's responsibility, that's going to mean that we give our children no less retirement security than we inherited from our parents. (Carol Moseley Braun)

437. Do not bring people in your life who weigh you down. And trust your instincts ... good relationships feel good. They feel right. They don't hurt. They're not painful. That's not just with somebody you want to marry, but it's with the friends that you choose. It's with the people you surround yourselves with. (Michelle Obama)

438. The last four or five hundred years of European contact with Africa produced a body of literature that presented Africa in a very bad light and Africans in very lurid terms. The reason for this had to do with the need to justify the slave trade and slavery. (Chinua Achebe)

439. I am where I am because of the bridges that I crossed. Sojourner Truth was a bridge. Harriet Tubman was a bridge. Ida B. Wells was a bridge. Madame C. J. Walker was a bridge. Fannie Lou Hamer was a bridge. (Oprah Winfrey)

440. There's a history of enslaved African-Americans having to make their slave masters comfortable. This business of

what we call skinning and grinning - that is something African-Americans are very much cognizant of. (Maxine Waters)

441. Never be limited by other people's limited imaginations. (Dr. Mae Jemison)

442. Though race-related issues continue to occupy a significant portion of our political discussion, and though there remain many unresolved racial issues in this nation, we, average Americans, simply do not talk enough with each other about things racial. (Eric Holder)

443. I've wrestled with alligators, I've tussled with a whale. I done handcuffed lightning. And throw thunder in jail. You know I'm bad. Just last week, I murdered a rock, injured a stone, hospitalised a brick. I'm so mean, I make medicine sick. (Muhammad Ali after 1974's *The Rumble in the Jungle*)

444. This nation has always struggled with how it was going to deal with poor people and people of color. Every few years you will see some great change in the way that they approach this. We've had the war on poverty that never really got into waging a real war on poverty. (Maxine Waters)

445. "If you're beefing at a wedding, why bring that to someone else's club? It's upsetting to me and my home girl because well damn if you can't go to Bella Noche, where the hell can you go?" (Hazel London)

446. We're not willing to give black leaders second chances because, in most cases, we're not willing to give them first

chances. (Al Sharpton)

447. Why should they ask me to put on a uniform and go ten thousand miles from home and drop bombs and bullets on brown people in Vietnam while so-called Negro people in Louisville are treated like dogs and denied simple human rights? (Muhammad Ali in 1966)

448. We're not Americans, we're Africans who happen to be in America. We were kidnapped and brought here against our will from Africa. We didn't land on Plymouth Rock – that rock landed on us. (Malcolm X)

449. God is not upset that Gandhi was not a Christian, because God is not a Christian! All of God's children and their different faiths help us to realize the immensity of God. (Desmond Tutu)

450. I always had a deep affection for Malcolm and felt that he had a great ability to put his finger on the existence and the root of the problem. He was an eloquent spokesman for his point of view and no one can honestly doubt that Malcolm had a great concern for the problems we face as a race. (Dr. Martin Luther King, Jr.)

451. I wouldn't be doing motherfu**ing films for almost three decades if every time I did something that someone didn't like I went in a fu**ing cocoon and just hid there and didn't make my art. (Spike Lee)

452. To change criminal justice policy in any meaningful way

means to propose changing a very longstanding system. It's not realistic to think you can do it overnight. (Kamala Harris)

453. We've come a long way in our thinking, but also in our moral decay. I can't imagine Dr. King watching the 'Real Housewives' or 'Jersey Shore.' (Samuel L. Jackson)

454. I'm a real person, and I'm angry. I'm trying to use this celebrity thing to get people some help. AIDS, poverty, racism - I want to be one of the hands that helps stop all that. I'll put it on my shoulders. I'll charge it to my account. (Jamie Foxx)

455. I will never change my name, because that's what I was born with (Quvenzhané Wallis)

456. how small, will grow into a mighty tree of refuge. We all want a future for ourselves and we must now care enough to create, nurture and secure a future for our children." (Afeni Shakur)

457. I don't much care who is gay or straight or married or not. I mostly notice if they are brave enough to confront bigotry. (Jasmine Guy)

458. We live in a society where manhood is all about conquering and violence. And what we don't realize is that ultimately that kind of manhood ultimately kills you. (Kevin Powell)

459. Failure: Is it a limitation? Bad timing? It's a lot of things. It's something you can't be afraid of, because you'll stop growing. The next step beyond failure could be your biggest success in life. (Debbie Allen)

460. We are still at the bottom of the pole after all these years. Even after having a black president. (Sean Combs in 2017)

461. The Negro is always to blame if some white woman decides she wants him. (Miles Davis)

462. If your hair is relaxed, white people are relaxed. If your hair is nappy, they're not happy. (Paul Mooney)

463. The United States is the most dishonest, ungodly, unspiritual nation that ever existed in the history of the planet. (Dick Gregory)

464. People in America worship money, and a white man's face on a green piece of paper does not make me wealthy. My health makes me wealthy. I used to work at a hospital, so I know the real deal. (Paul Mooney)

465. One thing that's true is that whether you are making a financial investment or an investment of the heart, you usually get what you give. What's also true is that investing the wrong assets into the wrong places is a great way to end up broke (or broken). (Dr. Boyce Watkins)

466. Now keep in mind that I'm an artist and I'm sensitive about my shit. (Erykah Badu)

467. Like comedy, horror has an ability to provoke thought and further the conversation on real social issues in a very powerful way. (Jordan Peele)

468. Being a part of this reemergence of a movement both pro-diversity and pro-woman is the best part of being a Black

girl. It's more than, "I stand for this because I should." I stand for this because this is part of who I am as a human being. (Yara Shahidi)

469. You don't start out writing good stuff. You start out writing crap and thinking it's good stuff, and then gradually you get better at it. That's why I say one of the most valuable traits is persistence. It's just so easy to give up! (Octavia Butler)

470. The norm is white, apparently, in the view of people who see things in that way. For them, the only reason you would introduce a black character is to introduce this kind of abnormality. Usually, it's because you're telling a story about racism or at least race. (Octavia Butler)

471. Poor is a state of mind you never grow out of, but being broke is just a temporary condition. (Dick Gregory)

472. I am the daughter of Nigerian immigrants. My mother is a survivor of both polio and of the Igbo genocide during her country's civil war in the late 1960s. Each Igbo name has a story behind it, so upon my birth, my mother carefully chose my name to be Uzoamaka, which means "the road is good." (Uzo Aduba)

473. I encourage everyone to pay attention to the issues that matter to you, from jobs and the economy, to education and our schools, to criminal justice reform. Whatever it is that you care about, make sure you use your voice. (2 Chainz)

474. The idea of 'talking white,' a lot of people grew up around

that, just the idea that if you speak with proper diction and come off as educated that it's not black and that it's actually anti-black and should be considered only something that white people would do. (Chance The Rapper)

475. People wanna say that they're part Native American or mixed, or anything other than black. We're raised to believe that there's something better about not being fully black, something eccentric about it. I'm saying I used to tell girls that I was mixed, which is a bold-faced lie! (Chance The Rapper)

476. It wasn't until I left that I realised it's not weird to grow up in certain cities and, by the age of 27 or 28, for all of your friends to still be alive. I can think of a lot of kids that I knew in Chicago who were supposed to grow up but didn't. (Chance The Rapper)

477. When I was nine years old, Star Trek came on, I looked at it and I went screaming through the house, 'Come here, mum, everybody, come quick, come quick, there's a black lady on television and she ain't no maid!' I knew right then and there I could be anything I wanted to be. (Whoopi Goldberg)

478. I absolutely reject the premise there is anything wrong with Black people "talking white". It is as if to vast swathes of the privileged white left and impoverished Black community diction, education and a mastery of thought is somehow

"white"... comrade, how wrong you are to say that after decades in academia I'm acting white. I'm being black. I'm being black everyday a cop pulls my car over for a "routine stop", I'm being black each time I look in the mirror, and I'm damn well being black when I school young fools out of the myth our race is too ill-evolved to be both black and accomplished. (Elaine Brown in 2008's *New Age Racism*)

479. You cannot look at the success of black people by seeing who is on the front of Ebony magazine or by looking at Oprah. When you consider that only 1 percent of all business revenue comes from black-owned businesses, you have to ask yourself if this class disparity is the kind of society we want. (Elaine Brown in a 2008 lecture at UCLA)

480. You don't want to think something might be racist, but it might be, because your gut is telling you it is. (Whoopi Goldberg)

481. We black men have a hard enough time in our own struggle for justice, and already have enough enemies as it is, to make the drastic mistake of attacking each other and adding more weight to an already unbearable load. (Malcolm X)

482. Black men loving black men is THE revolutionary act. (Marlon Riggs)

483. These two years have felt like hell and many sleepless nights, when I close my eyes to try to get some rest all I can see is my son getting shot. Our tax dollars are paying these

killer pigs. (Samira Rice in a 2016 speech demanding justice for the murder of her son Tamir Rice)

484. Racism is within each and every one of us. (Jordan Peele)

485. No matter how much money you have, no matter how famous you are, no matter how many people admire you, being black in America is — it's tough. And we got a long way to go for us as a society and for us as African-Americans until we feel equal in America. (Lebron James in 2017 after his home with vandalized with racial slurs)

486. I have been a slave myself -- I know what slaves feel -- I can tell by myself what other slaves feel, and by what they have told me. The man that says slaves be quite happy in slavery -- that they don't want to be free -- that man is either ignorant or a lying person. I never heard a slave say so. (Mary Prince)

487. I'm not hung up on this thing about liberating myself from the black man. I'm not going to try that thing. I got a black husband, six feet three, two hundred and forty pounds, with a fourteen shoe, that I don't want to be liberated from. (Fannie Lou Hamer)

488. Womanist is to feminist as purple to lavender. (Alice Walker)

489. The media wants to call them riots, but they're uprisings. Why should black people behave well to get their rights? White people don't behave and they get all the rights they

want. (Margo Jefferson)

490. Black people's music is in a class by itself and always has been. There's nothing like it. The reason for that is because it was not tampered with by white people. It was not on the media. It was not anywhere except where black people were. And it is one of the art forms in which black people decided what is good in it. Nobody told them. What surfaced and what floated to the top, were the giants and the best. (Toni Morrison)

491. Either black people end up being the best in sports, or else it's show business. You know, we all got rhythm. (Diana Ross)

492. Being an Other, in America, teaches you to imagine what can't imagine you. (Margo Jefferson)

493. You white women speak here of rights. I speak of wrongs. I as a colored woman have had in this country an education which has made me feel as if I were in the situation of Ishmael, my hands against every man, and every man's hand against me. (Frances Ellen Watkins Harper in 1866 speech *We're All Bound Up Together*)

494. When Negroes are average, they fail, unless they are very, very lucky. Now, if you're average and white, honey, you can go far. Just look at Dan Quayle. If that boy was colored he'd be washing dishes somewhere. (Bessie Delany in 1993's *Having Our Say*)

495. I hate it when, after I let a white person know they've said something racist, I end up having to listen for hours to their life. (Toi Derricotte)

496. Blacks are supposed to rejoice whenever our way of life becomes more mainstream. We seldom do. For we see in it a sanctioning that can only be granted by white society. In other words: If you're white, it's all right. If you're black, step back. (Lena Williams)

497. Being from the South, we never was taught much about our African heritage. The way everybody talked to us, everybody in Africa was savages and real stupid people. But I've seen more savage white folks here in America than I seen in Africa. I saw black men flying the airplanes, driving the buses, sitting behind the big desks in the bank, and just doing everything that I was used to seeing white people do. (Fannie Lou Hamer in 1964 after a trip to Africa)

498. Even today it is erroneously believed that all racial development among colored people has taken place since emancipation. It is impossible of belief for some, that little circles of educated men and women of color have existed since the Revolutionary War. (Pauline E. Hopkins in *Contending Forces: A Romance Illustrative of Negro Life North and South*)

499. Im a juicy peach but not everybody likes peaches. (Elexus Jionde)

500. White people cant ever let go of 9/11, a single day in our

history, but want you to get over 300 years of racial oppression lol. It really pisses me off that we are told we are ungrateful and trash Americans for not being happy docile niggers because slavery ended. Racists and "im not a racist but..." racists love to act like there wasn't a large period of racial motivated fuckery after slavery. (Elexus Jionde)

Made in the USA
Columbia, SC
05 May 2018